Charles Lempriere

The American Crisis

Charles Lempriere

The American Crisis

ISBN/EAN: 9783337378974

Printed in Europe, USA, Canada, Australia, Japan

Cover: Foto ©ninafisch / pixelio.de

More available books at **www.hansebooks.com**

THE AMERICAN CRISIS

CONSIDERED

BY

CHARLES LEMPRIERE, D.C.L.

OF THE INNER TEMPLE

LAW FELLOW OF ST. JOHN'S COLLEGE IN THE UNIVERSITY OF OXFORD

LONDON

LONGMAN, GREEN, LONGMAN, AND ROBERTS

1861

PREFACE.

Having no political bias, no object either personal or peculiar to serve, I have been induced to publish the opinion I have formed on these momentous questions, because I cannot satisfy myself that the facts published, and the articles written with the view of leading the public in England to a right and fair conclusion, have been certain or even veracious. The curious apparent vacillation of ideas which has prevailed, is, to say the least, suspicious that the facts have been made up to support them on one side or the other. My acquaintance with a vast number of American citizens in all four continents, and the opportunities I have had of hearing the opinions of every class and every kind of party, have led me to look carefully before I can honestly form conclusions upon questions so violently argued, as is invariably the case on the other side of the Atlantic. Civil war is fearful as well as slavery. But civil war, like other manslaughter, varies, according to circumstances, from murder to justifiable homicide; and I hardly think we in England are quite competent to decide on the question of slavery, as it exists in the Southern States, upon the evidence before us. At all events, no fair opportunity has yet been afforded them, either of explanation or of modification, of the recognised evil, in the face of the coercion and abolition which has been the policy of the ruling portion of the Northern statesmen for the last twenty years. *Errare humanum est.* I may be wrong, but the very difficulty I have experienced in sifting and understanding the reasons adduced by either side for their action in this crisis has been the moving cause of my humbly endeavouring to afford others an opportunity of at least knowing the arguments and facts to be found authenticated in these pages, and which appear to the writer to warrant the conclusions advanced.

5, Pump Court, Temple,
    Aug. 20, 1861.

CONTENTS.

THE AMERICAN CRISIS

CONSIDERED.

CHAPTER I.

THE CONSTITUTIONAL QUESTION.

THERE is, of course, to any European mind, a great difficulty in recognising the bearings of a constitutional question in a government so differently constituted from anybody politic on this side of the Atlantic as the United States are, more especially in the absence of any recognised work by which a standard of its form and constitution can be apprehended; but the very framework of the whole, in the original Declaration of Independence in 1776, the very name by which the nation chose to be designated, the facts which are abundant of the jealousy with which not only the whole nation, but also every individual State, and even every individual American, have guarded " consent " as being essential in some form or other to the free action of the Supreme Power,—all these prove incontestably that a right exists somewhere and somehow to control, and if necessary to controvert, the position of absolute authority. Now, as far as the exertion, and in many cases the success of resistance by separate States assuming, in so many words, to be sovereign against the action of government without the previous formal and legal " consent " of such State, can enable us to argue on this point of the question, this right of resistance resides in the legislative action of the States whether in each separately, or in the whole combined in Senate and Congress. And until the proposition that the Northern States are the government, and the Southern have no right to withdraw from it, is affirmed by both the one and the other, it appears conclusive that the legal and constitutional authority to act by armed force is deficient. Nor is it any answer to say that the President, being duly elected according to law, became *ipso facto* Governor of the country. He did not until he was accepted by the legislature both of the separate States and the whole combined, which we know has never been the case — and the deliberate action of Virginia by a vote of 150,000 majority — of North Carolina and Tennessee unanimously—all three claiming to be sovereign States, and on the express ground that the coercion proposed was not legal, proves that such was the view taken and acted on some time after the question had been fairly raised and discussed. Arkansas also, by the regular and constitutional exercise of her lawful powers, dissolved the connection. Kentucky, Maryland, and Missouri refused to join in coercing the Southern States on the same ground. Surely, without some strong authority, the force of which has never been disputed — the mere assertion in speeches and newspapers, that all this deliberate action is *rebellion*, cannot be accepted as having a legal or moral force with any one who has the slightest acquaintance with the political action of history. We have, as a fact, fourteen States openly dissolving the Union, and in a formal manner seceding from the general body of the nation. How, then, even in the popular view of vote by majority, can there remain a sufficient quorum to make up the constitutional number for a legislative act? We cannot, therefore, on all these grounds, resist the conclusion that, as a fact, the United States exist no longer; that there is no such government as the Union; and that the exercise of power as such, and on the supposition of a *status quo*, is unfounded in law and unsupported by any principle whether of national or general jurisprudence.

There cannot be a better illustration of the position I have laid down, that the power claimed and exercised, where possible, is a mere absolutism, acquiesced in because in accordance with the present feeling and bias of the masses, than the proceedings now taking place in Baltimore with regard to the forcible suspension of habeas corpus. Judge Tarney there plainly asserts that the President, by sanctioning the arrest of Merriman, and refusing to deliver him up on the writ of the judicature, " has trampled the laws of the country under foot," and I imagine few Englishmen would be found to gainsay it.

The whole course of the argument based on what is supposed to be the principle of the American constitution, results in this : that the consent of the people is requisite for every act and every form of government. What the peculiar force of State rights and Federal rights may be, depends apparently on individual cases, and have been the most fiercely argued, without any apparent definite solution but that the people are the source of all power, and that to them must inevitably be referred, as arbiters, every question of public policy, is the only tangible principle to be found. Until then the action of Government has been so indorsed and ratified it wants its proper stamp; and upon that and that alone depends the legality and sufficiency of its action. Does any one presume to assert that this has been done? The legislators and philosophers seem to take it for granted, that, in providing for the strength and greatness of the state they sufficiently provide for the happiness of the people, and cant about the duty of sacrificing everything to a country, the laws of which they will not permit to be peaceably put in force.

Senator Wade, of Ohio, declared, the evening the Kansas-Nebraska Bill passed, in 1854, " Henceforth there can be no political connection with the whigs of the South. An impassable gulf separates us. The North must pass under the yoke again. But not for long. No man can see the consequence of the deed about to be done. The future of the Republic is shrouded in gloom. All further compromises are at an end. The war must be carried on by the North with a resolute and uncompromising obstinacy, until things shall be put *in statu quo ante bellum.* I will appeal to the people and stimulate them to action, consoled by the assurance that if offences must come there is woe for those through whom they come."

Now, what is the inference to be drawn from all this assertion of rights and privileges of the free North? Why, surely, that these very gentlemen who are now ostensibly the leaders of public opinion in the Federal Government, who are most of them in actual office, and all of them the supporters of the Lincoln programme, not more than six years ago, openly advocated the doctrine, and advised the course on their own side of the question, which when taken by the other they denounce as treason, rebellion, and fratricide. Do they suppose the people of England cannot see these things, or if they see them will not heed?

Constitutionally speaking, according to the law of the United States, the Southern Confederation had an indefeasible right to withdraw from the Union, and had exercised that right legally. The position which the President assumed for the Northern section as constituting *the State*, and the Southern as *in rebellion*, is not founded either in fact or in reason. In plain truth, the exact expression is embodied in the witticism that the *United* States are become *Untied*. I now propose to test the proceedings of the Electoral Government in support of my proposition. Has there been any act of the legislature passed to define the relative

positions of the two contending sections? Not one.
Has there been any declaration or State paper
issued for the information of foreign Governments,
or, in fact, any other than their own dependents, as
to the rights claimed by the Government, the laws
violated by the seceding States, or the legal powers
by which the President and his Government are
authorised in restraining by armed force a resistance
against his rule? Not one. We are left to gather
all these most vital points from speeches delivered
irregularly, and often most obscurely worded, before
tumultuous meetings. All the acts done are solely
on the authority of the President *quâ* President of
the United States, by the plenary power of himself
alone, without any action of what in every people,
government, or nation under the sun is supposed
to represent the will of the body politic.* Even
the autocrats of Russia have never, in their proudest
day of power, wielded so despotic a sway. What,
then, is the secret of its easy adoption so far? It
is the taking the lead in the onward rush of the
mob, the embodiment into political action of the
passions which rage in the minds of the masses;
not the deliberate march of authority legally con-

* The Congress of 1861 begins by recognising this in passing an
Act to legalise the present proceedings up to the date of July.

stituted and judicially exercised. It is, in fact, force and not reason — anarchy and not law.

No allowance is made for the difficulties in which the question of emancipation is involved. These people totally forget that they have no right to interfere with the question, unless they are prepared to pay for the negro's freedom, and his master is willing to sell him. They foolishly expect to coerce the Southern people to uproot their social fabric, and for ever impoverish themselves and their posterity. Nay, more, they have the effrontery to offer such an argument as this :—

" The average value of land in the Southern States would have been, but for slavery, at least equal to the average value of the North; but land in the North is worth $28·07 an acre, and in the South, only $5·34 ; therefore, as there are 331,000,000 acres held by non-slaveholders in the South, their land is depreciated $22·73 per acre. The Southern domestic institution owes the country this difference, as the amount of the damage the land has sustained. Our claim is $7,544,148,825. It will not avail to parley or prevaricate; our claim is just and overdue; your criminal extravagance has almost ruined us ; we are determined you shall no longer play profligate, and fare sumptuously

(Helper spells it fair) everyday at our expense. But in order to show how brazenly absurd are the howls and groans you set up for compensation, whenever we speak of abolition, suppose your negroes worth what you ask, and that we are bound to secure you all that sum before they can be set free, the account stands,—

Non-slaveholders' account against slaveholders .	7,544,148,825
Slaveholders' account against non-slaveholders . .	1,600,000,000
	$5,944,148,825

So that, in truth, you have filched from us nearly five times the amount of the assessed value of your slaves.

" Out of our effects you have long since overpaid yourselves for your negroes; and now, sirs, you must emancipate them, and speedily, or we will emancipate them for you; and, correctly speaking, it will cost you nothing. You have a landed estate of 173,024,000 acres, at $5·34 per acre, present value, therefore $923,248,160. With the beauty and sunlight of freedom beaming on it, the estate would be worth, at $28·07 per acre, $4,856,783,680, so that the probable enhancement of value whenever you abolish would be thus :—

Estimate of lands after abolition .	.	.	.	4,856,783,680
Present value under slaves .	.	.	.	.	923.248,160
				$3,933,535,520

i. e. twice the estimated value of your negroes. So that by abolishing slavery you realise a nett profit of hundreds of millions of dollars. The hope of realising smaller sums has frequently induced men to perpetrate acts of injustice, we can see no reason why the certainty of becoming immensely rich in real estate, should make them falter in the performance of a sacred duty." *

And to place the alternative to such an equitable demand in such a form as this:—

" Again: small-pox is a nuisance; mad dogs are a nuisance; slavery is a nuisance; slaveholders are a nuisance; so are slave-breeders. It is our business, nay, it is our imperative duty to abate nuisances, therefore we propose to exterminate the catalogue from end to end. We are determined, we are wedded to one purpose, from which no earthly power can ever divorce us: to abolish slavery at all hazards, in defiance of all opposition of whatever nature which it is possible for slaveocrats to bring against us. Of this they may take due notice, and govern themselves accordingly." †

* Helper, p. 124.   † Ibid. p. 139.

" It is our honest conviction that the slaveowners by being responsible for the continuance of the baneful institution among us, deserve to be at once reduced to a parallel with the basest criminals that now lie fettered in the cells of our public prisons. Were it possible to gather into four equal gangs of licensed robbers, slaveowners, thieves, and murderers, society, we feel assured, would suffer less from their atrocities than it does now." *

" But, sirs, knights of bludgeons, chevaliers of bowie-knives and pistols, lords of the lash — particularly for five or six millions of Southern non-slaveholders, whom your iniquitous statism (what word is this?) has debarred from almost all the mental and material comforts of life,— we say you must emancipate and pay each slave at least sixty cash in hand, remunerating them at the rate of less than 26 cents per annum for the long and cheerless period of their servitude since August 20, 1620." †

" Compensation to slaveowners for negroes ! Preposterous idea, the suggestion is criminal, the demand unjust, wicked, monstrous, damnable. Shall we pat the bloodhounds for the sake of doing them a favour ? Shall we fee the curs of slavery to make them rich at our expense ? pay these whelps

* Helper, p. 158.   † Ibid. p. 185.

for the privilege of converting them into decent, honest, upright men?"*

Is not this fulfilling the warning: —

" *Washington's Farewell Address.*

" The constitution, which at any time exists till changed by an explicit and authentic act of the whole people, is sacredly obligatory upon all. The very idea of the power and the right of the people to establish Government presupposes the duty of every individual to obey the established Government.

" All obstructions to the execution of the laws; all combinations and associations, under whatever plausible character, with the real design to direct, control, counteract, or awe the regular deliberation and action of the constituted authorities, are destructive of this fundamental principle, and of fatal tendency. They serve to organise faction, to give it an artificial and extraordinary force, to put in the place of the delegated will of the nation the will of a party, often but a small but artful and enterprising minority of the community; and, according to the alternate triumphs of different parties, to make the public administration the mirror of the ill-concerted and incongruous projects of faction, rather than the

* Helper, p. 328.

organs of consistent and wholesome plans, digested by common councils, and modified by mutual interest.

" However combinations or associations of the above description may now and then answer popular ends, they are likely, in the course of time and things, to become potent engines by which cunning, ambitious, and unprincipled men will be enabled to subvert the power of the people, and to usurp for themselves the reins of Government, destroying afterwards the very engines which had lifted them to unjust dominion."

We feel that the best course to be pursued in this fatal controversy is to lay the arguments side by side for the opinion of any who may be left to hear the voice of reason amongst the passion and turmoil of civil strife. What is the actual state of things may be best seen by the following proclamation issued by Governor Jackson, explaining the relative position of the State and Federal Governments: —

"Jefferson City, June 12, 1861.

" To the People of Missouri : —

" A series of unprovoked and unparalleled outrages have been inflicted on the peace and dignity of this commonwealth, and upon the rights and liberties of its people, by wicked and unprincipled men, professing to act under the authority of the United States Government; the solemn enactments of your legislature have been nullified; your volunteer soldiers have been taken prisoners; your commerce with your sister States has been suspended; your trade with your own fellow-citizens has been and is subjected to increasing control of an armed soldiery; peaceful citizens have been imprisoned without warrant or law; unoffending and defenceless men, women, and children have been ruthlessly shot down and murdered, and other unbearable indignities have been heaped upon your State and yourselves. To all these outrages and indignities you have submitted with patriotic forbearance, which has only encouraged the perpetrators of these grievous wrongs to attempt still bolder and more daring usurpations.

" It has been my earnest endeavour, under all these embarrassing circumstances, to maintain the peace of the State, and avert, if possible, from our borders the desolating effects of civil war. With that object in view, I authorised Major-General Price, several weeks ago, to arrange with General Harney, commanding the Federal troops in this State, the terms of an agreement by which the peace of the State might be preserved. They came, on the 21st of May, to an understanding which was made public. The State authorities have laboured faithfully to carry out the terms of that agreement. The Federal Government, on the other hand, not only manifested its strong disapprobation of it by the instant dismissal of that distinguished officer, who, on its part, entered into it, but it at once began and has unintermittingly carried out a system of hostile operation, in utter contempt of that agreement, and in reckless disregard of its own pledged faith. The acts have latterly portended revolution and civil war so unmistakeably that I resolved to make one further effort to avert these dangers from you.

" I therefore solicited an interview with Brigadier-General Lyon, commanding the Federal army in Missouri. It was granted on the 11th instant, and, waving all questions of personal and official dignity, I went to St. Louis, accompanied by Major-General Price. We had an interview on the 11th instant with General Lyon and Colonel F. P. Blair, jun., at which I submitted to them these propositions: — 'That I would disband the State guard and break up its organisation; that I would disarm all the companies which had been ordered out by the State; that I would pledge myself not

to organise the militia under the military bill; that
no arms or munitions of war should be brought into
the State; that I would protect all citizens equally
in all their rights, regardless of their political opinions; that I would repress all insurrectionary movements within the State; that I would repel all
attempts made to invade it from whatever quarter,
and by whomsoever made, and that I would thus
maintain a strict neutrality in the present unhappy
contest, and preserve the peace of the State; and I
further proposed that I would, if necessary, invoke
the assistance of the United States troops to carry
out those pledges. All this I proposed to do upon
condition that the Federal Government would undertake to disarm the home guard, which it has
illegally organised and armed throughout the State,
and pledged itself not occupy with its troops any
localities in the State not occupied by them at this
time. Nothing but the most earnest desire to avert
the horrors of civil war from our beloved State
could have tempted me to propose these humiliating
terms. They were rejected by the Federal officers.
They demanded not only the disorganisation and
disarming of the State militia and the nullification
of the military bill, but they refused to disarm their
own home guard, and insisted that the Federal

Government should enjoy the unrestricted right to move and station its troops throughout the State whenever and wherever that might, in the opinion of its officers, be necessary, either for the protection of loyal subjects of the Federal Government, or for repelling invasion; and they plainly announced that it was the intention of the administration to take military occupation, under these pretexts, of the whole State, and reduce it, as avowed by General Lyon himself, to the exact condition of Maryland.

" The acceptance by me of those degrading terms would not only have sullied the honour of Missouri, but would have aroused the indignation of every brave citizen, and precipitated the very conflict which it has been my aim to prevent. We refused to accede to them, and the conference was broken up.

" Fellow-citizens, all our efforts towards concession have failed. We can hope nothing from the justice or moderation of the agents of the Federal Government in this State. They are energetically hastening the execution of their bloody and revolutionary schemes for the inauguration of civil war in your midst; for the military occupation of your State by so many bands of lawless invaders; for

the overthrow of your State government and for
the subversion of those liberties which the Government has always sought to protect; and they intend
to exert their whole power to subjugate you, if possible, to the military despotism which has usurped
the powers of the Federal Government.

"Now, therefore, I, C. F. Jackson, Governor of
the State of Missouri, do, in view of the foregoing
facts, and by virtue of the power vested in me by
the constitution and laws of this commonwealth,
issue this my proclamation, calling the militia of
this State, to the number of 50,000, into active
service of the State, for the purpose of repelling
such invasion, and for the protection of the lives,
liberties, and property of the citizens of this State;
and I earnestly exhort all good citizens of Missouri
to rally to the flag of their State for the protection
of their endangered homes and firesides, and for the
defence of their most sacred rights and dearest
liberties.

"In issuing this proclamation I hold it to be my
most solemn duty to remind you that Missouri is
still one of the United States, that the executive
department of the State Government does not arro-
gate to itself the power to disturb that relation.
That power has been wisely vested in the conven-

tion, which will, at the proper time, express your sovereign will; and that meanwhile it is your duty to obey all constitutional requirements of the Federal Government. But it is equally my duty to advise you that your first allegiance is due to your own State, and that you are under no obligation whatever to obey the unconstitutional edicts of the military despotism which has introduced itself at Washington, nor submit to the infamous and degrading sway of its wicked minions in this State. No brave-hearted Missourian will obey the one or submit to the other. Rise then, and drive out ignominiously the invaders who have dared to desecrate the soil which your labours have made fruitful, and which is consecrated by your homes — CLAIBORNE F. JACKSON."

The notion that was cherished for some time after the rupture that some means might be discovered of reconciling the contending sections has utterly and completely failed; and this from causes which were known and felt on the other side of the water, but have never yet found expression on this — partly from the hope naturally felt that the evil might not be irremediable, and partly from the dishonest way in which the writers in the public press, and the press itself, at least, for some time, have argued the views of the North, to the exclusion of those of the South, whose rights they have almost totally ignored. The question of abolition has been put forward invariably as the sole cause of disruption, in deference to the known feeling of England and Europe generally — whereas, there are far graver and deeper questions affecting the relations between the Northern and Southern States, which, for the last quarter of a century, have been antagonistic, and which have culminated to the present crisis. These we propose first to examine historically, and then to deduce reasons which preclude the hope of any fair or honourable settlement of the difference. In 1844 the Methodist Episcopal Church divided, the Northern section refusing to recognise the Southern on many grounds beside the question of slavery, and a feeling of bitterness arose which has never been appeased among the members of that community. I need not point out the refusal of admission to the State of Missouri, and the compromise which was ultimately effected — for its history is too familiar to require discussion — but only notice it in passing as one of the early causes of dissension. It has been uniformly felt by the South that in this, as in other cases, they had been unfairly dealt with by the legislature. In fact,

since the compromise, the admission of every State
south of Mason and Dixon's line has been systematically resisted by the Northern statesmen, in open
disregard of the plain bearing of the constitutional
law on this head. This has been the cause of end-
less strife and bloodshed on all the border questions,
when the votes of the settlers became of importance,
and involves too deeply-rooted antipathies and prejudices ever to allow of reconciliation.

The systematic interference of the Northern
proselytisers in the States south of the line was
looked on, and most fairly so, as illegal and unjustifiable, while the manner in which it was conducted
was as ruffianly as it was otherwise in defiance of all
law and reason. The impression, founded on many
years' experience, that so far from repressing or discountenancing such interference with the South,
and forcing on them, as it were, a tyranny, the
Northern statesmen took every opportunity of jus-
tifying what had been done, and sketching in no
vague colours plans of subjugation, and further
reducing into possession the Southern States, led all
thinking men of the latter party to see that unless
steps were taken at once to assert their independence their strength would be undermined. They
found emissaries were sent with incendiary papers

throughout the whole country — libels on the South were circulated throughout every town and hamlet, and especially in the schools. Not to go too far back, the first struggle for power, which illustrates the position of two sections, was the Fugitive Slave Law passed in 1850.*   This was, in fact, a compromise.   The state of enmity between the North and South had become so virulent, that such men as Clay, Webster, &c., saw that a disruption was inevitable.   They knew that, constitutionally, the South were right in resisting the open aggression of the North, and, morally, in defending their just title to the property which the law of the Union had guaranteed to them.   On the other hand, the present secretary of President Lincoln, W. H. Seward, in the debate brought forward what has since been characterised as the Higher Law Pressure, stating as his principle of action the obligation on his conscience from a higher law than that of the law of the land; a mode of statesmanship more in accordance with the politics of Cromwell's generals than has happily occurred in the annals of history since that day — for no one can possibly prognosticate whither the force of conscience can compel a fanatic.

Although the slave right was the question on

* See Webster's speech, March 7, 1850.

which the two parties came to an issue, on this as on other occasions, when they met in open conflict, it cannot be denied that the graveness of the offence was the unwarrantable assumption of the part of the North to override the rights of the South by an unconstitutional exercise of power, and that it was so is proved not only by the arguments of Daniel Webster, the ablest, as the most temperate, of modern American statesmen, but, also, most palpably by the direction events took in the consequent settlement of this question, as well as the subsequent presidential contests. Previous to 1850 the separate States of the North had resisted the resumption of a slave who had escaped from his master — fourteen of them had passed laws in their State Legislatures to that effect. To meet the complaint urged by the owners of slaves using the fair legal argument that the law of the land was bound to protect their property, Webster, Clay, and others brought in an Act to enable the slaveowner to pursue his slave into any State in the Union, and to call on the Federal authorities to assist him in recovering his property. Now, right or wrong, the law of the land did universally acknowledge the ownership of slaves, and the right accorded by this Act. " The Fugitive Slave Act " was affirmed by a majority in the Senate and in Congress after a long and bitter contest, and approved by Filmore, the then President. From this date commenced the disruption of the Union. The Federal officers, acting under this law, have been systematically resisted in the execution of their duty, even after the affirmation of it by the solemn judgment of the Supreme Court of Judicature of the United States.

In almost every case the expense and hindrance cost the owner more in recovering his slave than the property was worth, while in many he lost it altogether, and not seldom his life too, in the pursuit of it according to law. Now, however we may deplore and protest against the tenure of slaveholders, we cannot, by any principle known to civilised nations, ignore the fact, that the first duty a citizen owes the State is obedience to its laws, and resistance against their execution is an offence against the whole State. But in the United States not only was such resistance applauded by the Northern States, but it was made expressly the ground of asserting an unconstitutional supremacy over their equals in the Confederated Union. It was the injustice felt to be so done, and the right according to law which the South undoubtedly had, that swayed the nation in 1852, in their choice of Peirce—a New Hampshire candidate, who was in favour of carrying out the laws of the land — in preference to General Scott, the present commander of the Northern forces; and again, in 1856, in electing Buchanan, a Pennsylvanian, who avowed his intention of carrying out the law, by a large majority over Colonel Fremont. This proves incontestably that up to that date moderate and constitutional views prevailed in the body of the national electors; and the South, although they did not consider they had their full and fair share in the rights and privileges of the nation, yet acquiesced, in the hope that moderation and constitutional equity would guide the spirit of legislation.

The question of interest, which still more largely affects the motives which have induced both sides to hazard all their public and private ties, will be fully dealt with in a subsequent chapter. It is one which is totally ignored by every writer and speaker on the Federal side with a most patent unanimity — for they are aware how it tells against them. I shall for the present content myself with quoting a very late authority for my denial that the slavery question is sole element of this fearful disruption, and asserting that it is very far in importance behind another, which has been studiously kept in the background by the North.

" It is not slavery, but protection; it is not sentiment, but interest, which has destroyed the unity of the Great Transatlantic Republic.

"It is not any anxiety of New York to manumit the slaves, who raise the produce by which New York sends forth her volunteers, and makes her welcome them so warmly when they come back warworn at the end of three months' enlistment. The South, unless it were rich and productive as it lately was, would be of no use to New York.

" Nor is it the fear of danger to their 'domestic institutions' which gathers the Southern host at Manassas Gap.

"' It is,' says Mr. Bernal Osborne, quoting William Cobbett's prophecy, now thirty years old, 'because the heavy import duties on British goods are neither more nor less than so many millions a year taken from the Southern States, and given to their Northern competitor.'" *

Having thus endeavoured to show what appears to be the course of conduct which has caused the present disruption and future total disunion of the States of America, it only remains to consider what will be its effect upon England and the other powers of Europe. Commercially speaking, the opening of

* The "Times," August 10th, 1861.

direct trade with the cotton, rice, and tobacco producing countries, unfettered by a prohibitory tariff, will of course be an advantage. Nor can the blockade which shuts out the world from this trade be long suffered to stand in the way. How it will be broken it is impossible to say; but if the experience of history is to guide us in appreciating the spirit with which the United States deals with foreign nations, there will not long lack an excuse. It would be well for England and France to seize the present opportunity for inculcating the Confederate States with a more liberal legal policy in dealing with slavery, and, without interference or dictation, advise as friends a modification of its disabilities. There is no indisposition on their part to ameliorate the condition of their slaves; and where a spirit of conciliation in lieu of coercion, of sympathy in difficulty in lieu of an antagonism which threatens subjugation, suggests a course of policy which the sense of the civilised world approves, we have no doubt of a happy result to such intervention. We may add that the experience of the working of the law in Brazil, under similar circumstances, fully warrants such an anticipation.

Any other intervention is now happily out of the question; the Emperor Napoleon seems to be thoroughly in accord with the unanimous feeling of the people of this country, to keep out of this disastrous quarrel as long as it is possible to avoid it. But will it be always possible? Whatever ministry may hold the reins of office will know of a certainty at what price to value the abuse poured upon England by *statesmen* who require active co-operation from the subjects of a foreign government on a question of purely domestic interest. Our policy is quite assured,—to remain perfectly neutral until some outrageous act against our national honour, or against the law or interest of nations in general, compels us to assert our influence in arms. Let the Federal Government look to it that they do not so force us. Already there are manifest signs that the old rule of uncontrolled democratic action is at work. Violent men are crying out that enough has not been done, and that the country requires more energetic men and measures. The voice of sensible expostulation has been long hushed. The world trembles at the mutterings of a thunder which, in so many instances in Europe, has ushered in amongst the convulsions of empires the utter extinction of law, of commerce, and even of security for life itself.

CHAP. II.

THE NEGRO.

No one can deplore the bitterness of the contest raised by his self-constituted advocates with more justice than the slave himself. Unless the horrible and fearful anticipations of the abolition orators we have above noticed, be realised, and the whole wealth and intelligence of the southern portion of the United States be quenched in blood, his condition stands but little chance of amelioration from the efforts of his friends. What has been the result of emancipation without safeguards has been already published to the four quarters of the globe in such graphic terms that we make no apology for inserting them.

" In the United States there are 4,000,000 of these blacks, who, as slaves, are eminently useful to themselves and to humanity at large. To emancipate them is to convert 4,000,000 productive workers into as many idle paupers. Who is to support those paupers in their idleness, which with them is synonymous with freedom? In the West Indies they eat the spontaneous fruits of the earth; in the United States there are none for them to eat. That the blacks are now kept to work as northern white apprentices and paupers are kept to work, for their own and society's benefit, is true; in that respect the institution operates as a great workhouse, where the naturally idle are compelled to contribute their share to the services of mankind."

"The highest rewards, political and social, have been in the island of Jamaica vainly held out to the black to induce him to work. John Bigelow, Esq., in his letters to the *Evening Post*, afterwards embodied in a book on the condition of Jamaica, with the best intentions in the world to favour the black, showed conclusively that labour is the last thing he will undertake. The land is, if not the most prolific, at least as much so as any in the world. It may be bought from $5 to $10 per acre, and the possession of five acres confers the right of voting and eligibility to public offices. The planters offer freely $1·50 per day for labour; sixteen days' labour will buy such a piece of land, and the market of Kingston offers a great demand for vegetables at all times.

These facts, stated by Mr. Bigelow, place independence within the reach of every black, yet what are
the results? there has been no increase of black voters
in the last twenty years; the land runs wild; Kingston gets its vegetables from the United States, even
from New York; and 50,000 coolies have been imported to raise sugar on the plantations, the sensual
black, meanwhile, basking in the sun, and feeding on
yams and pumpkins. That is black nature. The
omnipotent Deity, who placed those blacks under
white control will not hold those guiltless who have
from hope of greater gain shirked from the responsibility of masters, and allowed them to sink back
to their savage condition."*

" There is no blinking the truth. Years of bitter
experience; years of hope deferred; of self-devotion
unrequited; of poverty; of humiliation; of prayers
unanswered; of suffering derided; of insults unresented; of contumely patiently endured, have
convinced us of the truth. It must be spoken out
loudly and energetically, despite the wild mockings
of 'howling cant.' The freed West India slave
will not till the soil for wages; the free son of
the ex-slave is as obstinate as his sire. He will
not cultivate lands which he has not bought for

* Trollope's " West India Islands."

his own.   Yams, mangoes, and plantains—those
satisfy his wants; he cares not for yours.   Cotton,
sugar, coffee, and tobacco he cares but little for.
And what matters it to him that the Englishman
has sunk his thousands and tens of thousands on
mills, machinery, and plant, which now totter on
the languishing estate that for years has only returned beggary and debt!   He eats his yams and
sniggers at buckra.

"We know not why this should be, but it is so.
The negro has been bought with a price—the
price of English taxation and English toil.   He
has been redeemed from bondage by the sweat and
travail of some millions of hard-working Englishmen.   Twenty millions of pounds sterling—one
hundred millions of dollars—have been distilled
from the brains and muscles of the free English labourer of every degree to fashion the West
India negro into a ' free and independent labourer.'
'Free and independent' enough he has become,
God knows; but labourer he is not, and, so far as
we can see, never will be.   He will sing hymns
and quote texts, but honest, steady industry he
not only detests but despises.   We wish to heaven
that some people in England—neither Government
people, nor parsons, nor clergymen, but some just-

minded, honest-hearted, and clear-sighted men —
would go out to some of the islands (say Jamaica,
Dominica, or Antigua*), not for a month, or three
months, but for a year, would watch the precious
protégé of English philanthropy, the freed negro,
in his daily habits; would watch him as he lazily
plants his little squatting, would see him as he
proudly rejects agricultural or domestic services,
or accept it only at wage ludicrously dispropor-
tionate to the value of his work. We wish too
they would watch him while, with a hide thicker
than a hippopotamus, and a body to which fervid
heat is a comfort rather than an annoyance, he
droningly lounges over the prescribed task, over
which the intrepid Englishman, uninured to the
burning sun, consumes his impatient energy, and
too often sacrifices his life. We wish they would
go out and view the negro in all the blazonry of
his idleness, his pride, his ingratitude, contemp-

* Nearly one-fourth part of the whole adult population of
Trinidad are returned by the last census as living in idleness.—
Lord Harris's despatch, May 18, 1852.

If we compare this with Great Britain, there are 250 persons
among the poor population of Trinidad to 8 among the wealthy of
Britain who are idlers. The difference is, the one race likes, and
the other hates, work ; and a people who will not work must be
slaves.

tuously sneering at the industry of that race which made him free, and then come home and teach the memorable lesson of their experience to the fanatics who have perverted him into what he is.

"Negroes, coolies, and planters—what is the position of each, and what are the rights of each? In England it is too much the custom to regard only the first of them. Floods of pathetic eloquence and long years of parliamentary struggling have taught us to imagine that the world was made for Sambo, and that the sole use of sugar is to sweeten Sambo's existence. The negro is, no doubt, a very amusing and a very amiable fellow, and we ought to wish him well; but he is also a lazy animal, without any foresight, and therefore requiring to be led and compelled. We must not judge him by ourselves. That he is capable of improvement everybody admits; but in the meantime he is decidedly inferior—he is but very little raised above a mere animal. The negroes know this themselves. They despise themselves. They know nothing of Africa, except that it is a term of reproach, and the name which offends them most is that of a nigger. So little confidence have they in any being who has an admixture of their blood, that no negro will serve a mulatto when he can serve a European

or a white creole. In his passion he calls the mulatto a nigger, and protests that he is not, never
will be, like buckra man. These coloured people
too despise themselves, and in every possible way
try to deny their African parentage. They talk
contemptuously of the pure blacks, whom they
describe as dirty niggers, and nasty niggers, and
mere niggers."*

" A servile race peculiarly fitted by nature for the
hardest physical work in a burning climate, the
negro has no desire for property strong enough to
induce him to labour with sustained power: he lives
from hand to mouth. In order that he may have his
dinner and some small finery, he will work a little;
but after that he is content to lie in the sun. This
in Jamaica he can very easily do; for emancipation and
free trade have combined to throw enormous tracts
of land out of cultivation, and on these the negro
squats, getting all that he wants with very little
trouble, and sinking in the most resolute fashion
back to the savage state. Lying under his cotton
tree, he refuses to work after ten o'clock in the
morning. ' No tankee, massa, me tired now; me
no want more money.' Or, by way of variety, he
may say, ' No, workee no more; money no 'nuff;

* " Times " leading articles.

workee no pay.'   And so the planter must see his cane foul with weeds because he cannot prevail on Sambo to earn a second shilling by going into the corn field. He calls him a lazy nigger, and threatens him with starvation. The answer is, ' No, massa, no starve now ; God sent plenty yam.' These yams, be it observed, on which Sambo relies, and on the strength of which he declines to work, are grown on the planter's own ground, and probably planted at his expense ; and Mr. Trollope suggests an inquiry into the feelings of an English farmer, if our labourers were to refuse work on the plea that there is plenty of potatoes and bacon to be had ; the potatoes and bacon being the produce of the farmer's own fields.   There lies the shiny, oily, odorous negro, under his mango-tree, eating the luscious fruit in the sun.   'He sends his black urchin up for a bread-fruit, and behold,' says Mr. Trollope, ' the family table is spread.   He pierces a cocoa-nut, and lo! there is his beverage.   He lies on the ground, surrounded by oranges, bananas, and pine apples. Why should he work? Let Sambo himself reply. ' No, massa, me weak in me belly ; me no work to-day; me no like workee; just 'em little moment.' "*

The same experience has been earned by the

* The " Times " on Trollope's " West India Islands."

French.   They emancipated their blacks when under the influence of the same delusion.   The same ruin attends their colonies.   A work of M. Vacherot, recently published in Paris, holds the following proposition in relation to the free black population of French Guiana:—

"The idlers should be punished by fine.   The small proprietor ought to be forced to produce in the same ratio in which he would do when working on a large estate at a salary.   The owner who will neither cultivate nor produce, is a vagabond to be punished.   It is not enough that he remains at home — that he begs from no one; he should be compelled to make the land he owns produce its share.   The landed vagabond is a greater nuisance than the wandering vagabond."

At the time of the adoption of the Federal constitution, the condition of slaves was very different at the South from what it has since become.   At that time there was no large branch of industry to engage, and their future fate was matter of anxiety.   The progress of the cotton culture has changed that, and the interests of millions of whites now depend upon the blacks.   The opinion of statesmen of that day were formed upon existing facts.   Could they have seen fifty years into the future their views upon black employment would have undergone an entire change. The blacks were then prospectively a burden; they are now an absolute necessity. They then threatened American civilisation; they are now its support. With multiplying numbers they have added to the national wealth. They have become the instruments of political agitation, while they have conferred wealth upon the masses. It is not the cotton alone that demands the slave labour, but sugar, tobacco and other interests require growing numbers of hands, for which there is no source of supply but natural increase. It is not, therefore, a matter of surprise that the blacks should be taken from the non-productive employments of the cities, and made to furnish the present profitable productions. The North exhibits a contrast to this, while the cities are overrun with poor who find no employment the West is destitute of hands for harvest. It is in vain that the papers preach to the " free labourers " the importance and benefit of farm labour. They cling to the cities, crowd tenement houses, and raise numbers of pauper children, which in New York, to some extent, are collected in benevolent institutions, sent West, and " bound out " to farmers for some years. Thus, on a small scale, goes on at the North what is found so generally necessary at the South.

But the South does not seek to force, or even intrude, their system on the North. They are excluded, justly, wisely, and contentedly from all political power and responsibility in your capital States. They are sovereigns on the subject of slavery within their own borders, as the North are on the same subject within their own borders. It is well and wisely so arranged. Use authority to maintain what system you please, they are not distrustful of the result. They have exercised theirs to protect and perfect the manhood of the members of the States. The whole sovereignty upon domestic concerns within the Union is divided between North and South by unmistakeable boundaries. The North have fifteen distinct parts; the South eighteen parts, equally distinct. Each must be maintained in order that the whole may be preserved. If one shall be assailed, within or without, by any enemy, or for any cause, and should it need, all will expect both North and South to defend it. If one shall be assailed, in the emergency, no matter what the cause or the pretext, or who the foe, the South will defend the sovereignty of the North as the equivalent of their own. They cannot, indeed, accept their system of capital or its ethics. That would be to surrender and subvert their own, which they esteem to be better. Besides, if they could, what need for any division into States at all? The North are equally at liberty to reject the system of the South and its ethics, and to maintain the superiority of their own by all the forces of persuasion and argument. The nation must, indeed, mutually discuss both systems. Especially must they discuss them, when they have to decide as a nation which of the two they ought to ingraft on the new and future states growing up in the great public domain. Discussion, then, being unavoidable, what could be more wise than to conduct it with mutual toleration and in a fraternal spirit?

The question of slavery in the territories settled itself according to the adaptation of the soil to slave labour. This is not a matter of sentiment or surmise, it is simply a matter of experience and history. The whole of the Northern free States were once " the homes of slavery." They all possessed that " property," and they all gradually abandoned it as of no practical value. This process is now going on in the Northern slave States. We may see in the table that the free negroes in Delaware were as 1 to 2 of the slaves in 1790, and as 9 to 1 in 1851. In Maryland the free blacks were to the slaves, in 1790, as 1 to 13; and in 1851 they were as 1 to $1\frac{1}{6}$. In Virginia they rose from 1 to 20 to 1 to $8\frac{1}{2}$. Nine States holding slaves in 1709 abolished the institution within thirty years of that date. The reason for doing so was not philanthropic nor yet political, but simply a matter of dollars and cents. Slave labour in that region was not worth having. This economical principle it is which governs slavery in the territories. Slavery will not go on to any of the present unappropriated territory of the nation, for the reason that it would not be profitable to go there, if it should so it would be certain to lose; because the future States would abolish the institution on account of its inutility; and would, like Ohio, Illinois, Indiana, and Minnesota, forbid blacks from coming in at all, either bond or free. These are fixed and well-known principles, and when a party of political hucksters profess only " one policy," that of keeping slavery out by virtue of their acts, they profess only a bald sham, which is an insult to the intelligence of the people, whose votes they seek. As well might a party of political traders point to the influx and efflux of the tide, and pretend that their efforts alone prevent the farm-lands on the Atlantic from being drowned at each recurring flood.

Barefaced as would be such an assumption, it is not more baseless than the pretence that Kansas was "saved to freedom" by Brown and Beecher. There is no man of intelligence who does not know that if Kansas had been made a slave State, and any number of slaves had been carried into it, that a very short time only would elapse before those slaves would have been emancipated by State laws, and consequently "freedom" would have gained instead of losing. If, then, we are to believe the assertion of the Republican leader, the now Secretary of State, "one policy" only "of which he knows" is a gross deception. It has no practical force or meaning beyond its use as a means of irritating the popular mind, in order to turn votes to the party, on the strength of that exasperation; yet he denominates this sham " the great national issue between free labour and capital labour for the territories," that parties are " conducting to its inevitable solution."

From the moment of the formation of the Federal Union there commenced a struggle for political power which has not ceased to be directed against the slave States. The instrument of union, while it provided for the extinction of the slave trade, which then formed so large a portion of Northern traffic, contained also a provision for black representation in the Southern States, stipulating that that representation should not be changed until 1808, and thereafter only by a vote of three-fourths of all the States. That provision has been the groundwork of that constant Northern aggression upon Southern interests, which has so successfully gained on the Federal power until now it imagines the desired three-fourths is within its reach, when the South, with its interests, will be at the feet of the abolitionists. The South has stood steadily on its defence, but while the circle has narrowed in upon it the North has not ceased to clamour against Southern aggression.

No sooner had the constitution been adopted, however, than the annexation of Louisiana became a necessity, in order to give an outlet to the sea for the produce of the West, but notwithstanding the great advantage which the annexation was to confer upon Massachusetts, she opposed it to the point of threatening to dissolve the Union if it was carried out. This, after the great rebellion of Shay, within her borders, was the first disunion threat, and the motive was fear of the political increase of Southern strength. Those fears were like all party pretences, short-sighted, since that territory has given more free than slave States to the Union. This threat of disunion was made while yet Massachusetts was engaged in

the slave trade, that the State had voted to prolong
to 1808.   The same cry was renewed in respect to
Florida, and again, with greater violence, in the case
of Missouri; to be again revived in respect of Texas;
and once more, with circumstances of greater atro-
city, in the case of Kansas.   It is remarkable that
while free States come in without any great
struggle on the part of the South, the safety of
which is threatened by each such accession, the admission of slave States is the signal of so much strife,
and this resistance to a manifest right of the South is
denounced as " Southern aggression."

The gradual abolition of slavery in the old Northern States and the rapidity with which eastern
capital, following migration, has settled the Western
States, has given a large preponderance to the free
interest in the national councils.   Of the twenty-six
senators that sat in the first Congress, all represented
a slave interest, more or less.   With the States and
territories now knocking for admission, there are
seventy-two senators, of whom thirty-two only represent the slave interest; that interest from being
" an unit" in the Senate, has sunk to a minority of
four, and yet the majority do not cease to complain
of Southern "aggression."   With this rapid decline
in the Southern vote in the great " Conservative

Body " of the Senate, the representation in the lower house has fallen to one-third. How long will it be before the desired three-fourths vote, for which a large party pant, will have been obtained, and when obtained what will have become of those Southern rights which are even now denied by party leaders to be any rights at all? In the last thirty years eleven free States have been prepared for the Union; a similar progress in the next thirty years and the South will have fallen into that constitutional minority which may deprive it of all reserved rights. This circle is closing rapidly in upon it, amid a continually rising cry of abolition, pointed by bloody inroads of armed men. This is called Southern " aggression."

The census of 1850 gave the nativities of the white population. The emigrants and their descendants number 5,000,000 souls, or one-fifth of the entire white population, and these have swollen the free State representation; while the population of the South, as well black as white, has progressed only by natural means. It is to be borne in mind, also, that the very prosperity of the South, growing out of large crops, and higher prices for it, operates against the political extension of the section, since it tends powerfully to concentrate the population. We shall show, under the head of cotton culture, the remarkable extension which took place during the speculative excitement, from 1830 to 1840, in the black population. The fertile lands of the great valley were then discovered to bear more cotton at less price than the Atlantic States, and that migration of blacks took place which produced so manifest a change in the slave population in the several States by the census of 1850. In the table of black population, of the blacks who left the Atlantic for the new States, a considerable number, when the disasters came on, were run to Texas; when that State was re-annexed, these slaves again appeared in the enumeration of 1850. The effects of that migration are very remarkable. In Delaware and Maryland the slave population fell from 106,286 in 1830, to 92,342 in 1840, a decline of 13,944 in addition to the natural increase. The free blacks in the same time increased 10,204. The census of 1850 gave a slight increase of slaves in that year. In the State of Virginia the slaves declined over 20,000 up to 1840, but recovered 23,000 up to 1850. In the nine years that have elapsed since the census, an immense addition has been made to the cotton crop, and also to its value. Although the crop doubled from 1830 to 1840, under the spur of the speculation of those years, it remained nearly stationary in the ten years up to 1850, since then it has again doubled; that is to say, the cotton raised in the five years ending with 1860 is 17,732,307 bales, and in the five years ending with 1850 there were raised 8,951,587, or 85,434 bales less than half, at the same time the price per pound at one time, in 1857, ranged 18 cents. Under such circumstances the value of cotton hands reached $2000; while they were nearly as valuable for sugar culture. It is obvious that, under such circumstances, no one can spare blacks for the settlement of new States. On the other hand, they are concentrated on the cotton lands of the old States with great rapidity, and the census of the next year will show the effects of those influences upon the local populations.

What then is to be done with them? for they exist, and we cannot blink the question. It is clear that simple manumission will not do, as the experiment has thoroughly failed. Whether a scale of fair wage for fair labour may ultimately be found seems but a philosopher's dream. Certainly, it is not likely to be realised by the present proceedings. We in England have suffered too much and too recently not to make the name of slave abhorent to every ear —but I should much like to know what the slaves think of it themselves. Certainly, their relative position in the North and South of the States tells

most unquestionably in favour of the latter in the
comfort and standing of the black.   Whether sup-
posing for a moment our English view of making
them free labourers, under certain restrictions and
compulsion, were carried out, the American white
man would tolerate their presence and communion
in any manner conducive to their comfort and self-
respect, is rendered very doubtful by the laws passed
by Indiana, Illinois, Oregon, Minnesota, Missouri, and
other Northern States, prohibiting their immigration,
and the patent disgust and seclusion with which they
are invariably and universally treated in the North.
Thus we find in Philadelphia 20,000 free negroes,
of whom 5000 are paupers, and the rest but little
credit to any civilised community; few of them pur-
suing any recognised occupation or creditable means
of earning a livelihood.   The same state of things I
have witnessed in Boston and New York.   In
Thompson Street the property is rendered almost
valueless by being occupied by free negroes, who
beg the coldest days of an almost arctic winter bare-
footed, and in the most abject state of misery.   In
the Northern States the fact is indisputable that the
negro is not cared for, and has no estate or provision
recognised by law or in society, but forced into degradation and want without chance or hope of escape.

On the other hand, throughout the Southern States, apart from the question of slavery, the negro has a recognised and comfortable position in society. He is provided and cared for by law, and is confessedly the happiest and merriest of mortals in any subordinate capacity. Were it worth while or without danger of exciting prejudices likely to interfere with the temperate and calm argument which befits the consideration of such a momentous subject as we have taken up, I might enlarge to almost any extent on the affectionate and child-like nature of the negro, which peculiarly fits him for the situation he holds towards a master who treats him with kindness and consideration; but I forbear, from the knowledge I have that the very mention of the relation brings with it the whole source of the bitterness that has brought communities living under one law and one government, rejoicing in a common name and common lineage, and that one of the proudest and noblest on the surface of the globe, to such a state of suicidal war, as to threaten not only the disruption of the community, for that is inevitable, but the social and commercial ruin of each, and not improbable, the almost total destruction of both, unless the merciful hand of God interfere to prevent so dire a catastrophe.

CHAP. III.

COTTON.

THE question of cotton is one that vitally interests the whole commercial world, and I propose shortly to review from the most authentic details some of its leading features and statistics.

The cotton growers of the Southern States do not regard with the slightest anxiety or jealousy the efforts that are being made to produce cotton in Asia, Africa, Australia, and South America. If success attends the movements of the Cotton Supply Association of Manchester, the result will be simply to enable the people of those countries to consume a quantity of manufactured goods in proportion to the quality of cotton produced and exported. It is a perfectly well-ascertained fact, that the cotton States of the Southern Confederacy contain the only cotton-growing region in the world, where more cotton is produced than is consumed in manu-

* For almost the whole details of this subject I am indebted to the kindness of J. P. Kettell, Esq., author of " Southern Wealth and Northern Profits."

factured goods. The hand labour of India and China cannot compete with the skilled industry of the manufacturing countries of Europe. India now receives from England almost twice the number of pounds of manufactured goods that she sends of raw cotton to England. In 1858 England received from India 132,722,575 lbs. of raw cotton, and sent to India 223,000,000 lbs. of yarns and manufactured cotton goods. As the trade of China is now thrown open, the fabrics of her hand-looms must give place to the machine goods of western Europe. If her consumption of cotton shall equal that of France, it will be 1,440,000,000 lbs., equal to 2,880,000 bales, of 500 lbs. each, per annum.

As much science is required and employed in the cotton culture as in any branch of agriculture in the world. But it is said cotton grows on trees in the tropics! So do grapes; but does it follow that the people of India and Africa can rival those of France in the cultivation of the vine? With improved implements and machinery, and the employment of horses, mules, and oxen, the quantity of cotton produced to the hand or labourer, has been more than doubled within the last twenty-five years. The quality has been improved by the selection of seed, and the improvement of the soil, by fertilisers and scientific culture.

Such has been the improvement in the cotton culture since 1852, that the number of acres which each labourer can cultivate, and the produce per acre, has been largely increased, and the quality of the staple or fibre very much improved. The cotton which was produced thirty years ago would not now be marketable. Under the improved system a labourer will now cultivate twenty acres of cotton with as much ease as he formerly culti-vated ten. Immense tracts of country that, ten years ago, were not considered sufficiently fertile for the profitable production of cotton, are being cultivated with perfect success. The area of land now regarded as valuable for cotton is more than five times larger than that stated in the census returns of 1850.

Cotton cannot be successfully produced further south than where there is sufficient frost to destroy the insects, which are so destructive to the plant in the tropics, and which, many years ago, caused its cultivation in the West Indies to be almost discontinued. The northern limit to which the culture may be carried is near the thirty-fourth degree of north latitude. That, however, depends on the elevation of the surface above the level of the sea—the mountain range being too cold. The southern limit of safe and profitable culture is from the twenty-ninth to the thirtieth degree of north latitude. These limits give a belt of about five degrees of latitude, in width extending from the Atlantic coast to the commencement of the elevated plains east of the Rocky Mountains. Cotton cannot be successfully cultivated in any region where there is a wet and dry season. The extremes of rain and drought are equally fatal to the production of the staple or fibre. Tropical rains cause the plant to grow too large, and either extreme wet or dry weather will cause the blossoms and young bolls to drop off. Therefore, climate is one of the first considerations in the selection of a region suitable for the cultivation of the cotton plant. That of the cotton states is peculiarly suitable for that purpose. The prevailing winds in spring and summer, charged with moisture, flow inland from the Atlantic, and are met by cold currents of air from the Alleghany and Rocky Mountains, which are attracted by the radiation of heat on the plains. The contact causes frequent showers of rain to fall throughout the spring, summer, and autumn, in sufficient quantity to preserve a healthy growth and early maturity of the plant, without endangering its product of cotton.

The principal cotton-producing States are: North Carolina, South Carolina, Georgia, Florida, Tennessec, Arkansas, Alabama, Mississippi, Louisiana, and Texas. The area of those States is 706,288 square miles, or 452,024,320 acres. The average product of cotton per acre is estimated at half a bale of 500 lbs. The crop of 1859, the largest yet made, was 4,500,000 bales, which at the average product required only 9,000,000 acres. It has been estimated that one half the area of the States named, is suited to the cultivation of cotton; but for the purpose of avoiding all possible criticism, I will say one-third, or 150,674,773 acres, which at half a bale to the acre, will produce 75,337,338 bales of 500 lbs. each, and the entire weight of which would be 37,668,673,000 lbs. If we assume that the entire population of the earth amounts to 1,200,000,000, that quantity of cotton would give $3\frac{1}{2}$ lbs. to every man, woman, and child on the face of the globe. This would be more than three times as much as is consumed in England, and nearly eight times the quantity consumed in France per head of the population. The consumption of Great Britain is stated to be 9 lbs., and that of France to be 4 lbs. per head of the entire population. If the consumption of the whole people of the world were to be brought up to the present consumption of France, they would require but 9,600,000 bales, or less than one-eighth part of the crop which the cotton States could produce. If the consumption were to reach that of Great Britain, it would require. 21,600,000 bales, or a little more than one-fourth of the capital for production of the cotton States.

When the cotton-gin of Whitney laid out the future work of the blacks, the steam engine of Watt, and the jenny of Hargrave, with the improvements of Arkwright and Crompton, laid out the future manufacturing industry of England and the mode of employing her capital. The old mode of preparing the cleaned cotton for spinning was by carding it between two flat cards in the hand of an individual, in order to straighten out the fibres as much as possible. The material so carded was spun by a wheel worked with one hand to give velocity to a single spindle that spun a thread from the cotton held upon a distaff in the left hand of the operator. The thread thus produced was irregular, and served only as a woof for linen warp. By a new invention, the cards were placed upon a revolving drum, which operated against several rollers, also covered with cards. The action of these rollers distributed the cotton in a fleecy web upon the surface. This was removed from the last roller by an instrument which caused the cotton to come off in long rolls ready for spinning. Arkwright added rollers that were to " draw " these rolls as they were carded, so as, by making the fibres of cotton more parallel to each other, to increase the fineness and regularity of the thread. The invention of Hargrave in 1764, was to put eight spindles in a frame, and draw the ends in a clasp held by the operator. The number was soon raised to eighty spindles. Samuel Crompton in 1779 added the "mule spinner." The effect of all these inventions was that, whereas one man could clean one pound of cotton, another card it, and another work one spindle; one man might now clean 360 lbs., another card it, and the third work 2200 spindles instead of one.

The English inventions were previous to the American invention of the gin, and their utility depended altogether upon the latter. The anxiety then took possession of the mind of the English manufacturer in relation to a supply of material which now, after seventy years, is as active as ever. Hitherto the demand has, as we have seen, developed black industry.

From that moment the accumulated capital of England, New and Old, became engaged in the gigantic operation of clothing the world with cotton. Hand-loom goods were everywhere to be supplanted by those formed on the new principle. When Watt started his engine, mechanical genius seemed to have sprung suddenly into life, and each subsequent year witnessed some improvement in machinery, by which the texture of the cloth has been improved and its cost diminished. Chemistry has as rapidly multiplied the number and richness of colours. The art of applying them by steel dies and copper cylinders has improved, until sixteen colours are imparted at one impression more perfectly than was one forty years ago; and the perfection of the designs is equalled only by the excellence of the execution. With each improvement in texture, and design, and colours, the fabric is produced at less cost, because a class of persons who formerly did not produce at all are now the chief manufacturers.

" 1. The finest long cotton in the world is called the ' Sea Island.' It is grown on the low-lying lands and small islands on the coast of Georgia. The quantity is small, and the price very high. It is used mostly for muslin thread, and the very finest number of yarn — say 100's and upwards — price, in fact is of little moment to the manufacturers who purchase it. It usually sells at about 2s. per pound. A quality much resembling it, and almost, if not quite as good, has been grown, as a sample article, in Australia. But of this denomination of cotton the consumption is very small. Another species, long, strong, fine, and yellowish, is grown in Egypt, and imported in considerable quantities. An inferior quality, coarse, harsh, bright in colour, but strong, is imported from Brazil, and a very small quantity from the West Indies. Doubtless if the price were adequate, and the demand here very great and steady, the supply from many of these quarters might be largely augmented. But it is not of this sort that we need any considerable increase, nor could we afford the price which probably alone would remunerate the grower.

" 2. Our great consumption and demand is for the soft, white, silky, moderately long cotton of America, the quality usually called ' Uplands,' ' Bowed Georgia,' and ' New Orleans.' This used to be sold at prices varying from 3*d.* to 6*d.* per pound (it is now from 6*d.* to 8*d.*); it can be consumed in any quantity, for it is available, not only for weft, but for warp, except for the finer numbers. We need and consume nine bags of this cotton for one bag of all other qualities put together.

" 3. It is the insufficient supply or the higher price of this cotton that has driven our manufacturers upon the short-stapled native article of India, commonly called Surat. If the price of the two were equal, scarcely a bag of Surat would be employed. When the price of American cotton rises, owing to an inadequate supply, that of East India cotton follows it at a considerable interval — the usual ratio being two to three — and the import of the latter is greatly stimulated. It is always grown in India in large quantities, and with improved means of communication, and more careful preparation, might be supplied in time in indefinite and probably ample quantities. But it is its quality that is in fault; and as far as the past is a guide, it would seem incurably in fault. Many attempts to amend the character of this cotton have been made: American planters and American 'saw-gins' have been sent over, and American seed has been planted, and the result has been a sensible amelioration in cleanliness and colour, and some slight increase in length of fibre, but scarcely any change in specific character. The dry, fuzzy, woolly characteristics remain. Sometimes the first year's samples nearly resemble the American article, but the resemblance never becomes permanent. Hitherto (we believe we are correct in stating), either from the peculiarity of the soil or of the climate, or as some say, from adulteration by the air-borne pollen of the inferior native plant, the improved and altered character of the cotton has never been kept up.

" We are far from saying that this difficulty may not be overcome, and American cotton be naturalised in our East Indian possessions; but certainly the results of our past efforts have not been of favourable augury. So far as our own observation and experience have gone, only from two other parts of the world have we seen samples of cotton analogous in character to that of the United States, and equally available for our purposes: one of these was the west coast of Africa, where we understand there is a considerable native growth, which doubtless our commerce might encourage and increase; the other is the opposite side of the continent, where Port Natal has exported some very hopeful samples, soft and silky, but not clean, nor of a very good colour, but still decidedly American in quality.

" The point we have to bear in mind then, is this: our desideratum is not simply more cotton, but more cotton of the same character and price as that now imported from the States. If India were to send us two millions of bales of Surat cotton per annum, the desideratum would not be supplied, and our perilous problem would be still involved. We should be almost as dependent on America as ever."*

The "London Cotton Supply Reporter" of Feb. 3rd, remarks:—

"Upwards of 500,000 workers are now employed in our cotton factories, and it has been estimated that at least 4,000,000 persons in the country are dependent upon the cotton trade for subsistence. A century ago Lancashire contained a population of only 300,000 persons; it now numbers 2,300,000. In the same period of time, this enormous increase exceeds that on any other equal surface of the globe, and is entirely owing to the development of the cotton trade. In 1856 there were in the United Kingdom 2210 factories, running 28,000,000 spindles, and 209,000 looms, by 97,000 horse power. Since that period a considerable number of new mills have been erected, and extensive additions have been made to the spinning and weaving machinery of those previously in existence.

"The amount of actual capital invested in the cotton trade of this kingdom is estimated to be between £60,000,000 and £70,000,000 sterling.

"The quantity of cotton imported into this

* J. B. Smith, Esq., M.P. for Stockport. Paper in the Journal of the Society of Arts.

country in 1859 was 1,181,750,000 lbs. weight, the value of which at 6*d*. per pound is equal to £30,000,000 sterling ; but of 2,829,110 bales of cotton imported into Great Britain, America has supplied us with 2,086,341 — that is, 5-7ths of the whole. In other words, out of every 7 lbs. imported from all countries into Great Britain, America has supplied 5 lbs. ; India has sent us about 500,000 bales ; Egypt about 100,000 ; South America 124,000 ; and other countries between 8000 and 9000 bales. In 1859 the total value of the exports from Great Britain amounted to £130,513,185, of which £47,020,920 consisted of cotton goods and yarns. Thus more than one-third, or £1 out of every £3 of our entire exports consists of cotton. Add to this the proportion of cotton which forms part of £12,000,000 more exported in the shape of mixed woollens, haberdashery, millinery, silks, apparel, and slops. Great Britain alone consumes annually £24,000,000 worth of cotton goods. Two conclusions, therefore, may safely be drawn from the facts and figures now cited: first, that the interests of every cotton worker are bound up with a gigantic trade which keeps in motion an enormous mass of capital, and this capital, machinery, and labour depend for 5-7ths of its employment upon the slave States of America for prosperity and continuance; secondly, that if a war should at any time break out between England and America, a general insurrection take place among the slaves, disease sweep off those slaves by death, or the cotton crop fall short in quantity, whether from severe frosts, disease of the plant, or other possible causes, our mills would be stopped for want of cotton, employers would be ruined, and famine would stalk abroad among the hundreds and thousands of workpeople who are at present fortunately well employed.

"Calculate the consequences for yourself. Imagine a dearth of cotton, and you may picture the horrors of such a calamity from the scenes you may possibly have witnessed when the mills have only run on 'short time.' Count up all the trades that are kept going out of the wages of the working classes, independent of builders, mechanics, engineers, colliers, &c., employed by the millowners. Railways would cease to pay, and our ships would lie rotting in their ports, should a scarcity of the raw material for manufacture overtake us."

It is not an inconsistency, therefore, that while we see only cause of congratulation in this wonderful increase of trade, Lord Brougham sees in it the exaggeration of an evil he never ceases to deplore.

We, and such as we, who are content to look upon society as Providence allows it to exist—to mend it when we can, but not to distress ourselves immoderately for evils which are not of our creation — we see only the free and intelligent English families who thrive upon the wages which these cotton bales produce. Lord Brougham sees only the black labourers who, on the other side of the Atlantic, pick the cotton pods in slavery. Lord Brougham deplores that in this tremendous importation of a thousand millions of pounds of cotton, the lion's share of the profit goes to the United States, and has been produced by slave labour. Instead of twenty-three millions, the United States now send us eight hundred and thirty millions, and this is all cultivated by slaves. It is very sad that this should be so, but we do not see our way to a remedy. There seems to be rather a chance of its becoming worse. If France, who is already moving onwards in a restless, purblind state, should open her eyes wide; should give herself fair play by accepting our coals, iron, and machinery; and under the stimulus of a wholesome competition, should take to manufacturing upon a large scale, then these three millions will not be enough. France will be competing with us in the foreign cotton markets, stimulating still further the produce of Georgia and South Carolina. The jump which the consumption of cotton in England has just made is but a single leap, which may be repeated indefinitely. There are a thousand millions of mankind upon the globe, all of whom can be most comfortably clad in cotton. Every year new tribes and nations are added to the category of cotton wearers. There is every reason to believe that the supply of this universal necessity will for many years yet to come fail to keep pace with the demand; and, in the interest of that large class of our countrymen to whom cotton is bread, we must continue to hope that the United States will be able to supply us in years to come with twice as much as we bought of them in years past.

We know very well that the possibility of growing cotton is not confined to the New World. The plains of Bengal grew cotton before Columbus was born, and we, with our mechanical advantages, can actually afford to take the Bengal cotton from the growers, and send it back to them in yarns and pieces cheaper than they can make it up. So, also, thousands of square miles in China are covered by the cotton plant; and some day we may, perhaps, repeat the same process there. Africa, too, promises us cotton. Dr. Livingstone found a country in

which the growth was indigenous, and where the
chiefs were very anxious to be taught how to cultivate it for a European market. There is no lack
of lands and climate where cotton could be produced.
It is said of gold that no substance in nature is
more widely diffused, and more omnipresent; but,
unfortunately, it is diffused under conditions which
make it seldom possible to win it with a profit.
So it is of cotton. The conditions under which it
becomes available for our markets are not often
present in the wild cotton which our travellers dis-
cover, nor are they to be immediately supplied.
Remember the efforts which the French have made
to produce cotton in Algeria, the enormous prizes
they offered, the prices at which they bought up
all the produce, the care with which fabrics were
prepared from these cottons at Rouen, and exhibited
at the Paris exhibition, and then note the miserable
result after so many years of artificial protection.
It will come eventually; as the cotton wants of the
world press heavily and more heavily, it must come.
We shall have cotton from India, from China, and
from Africa; we would advocate every means within
reasonable limits to quicken the development. We
would not even ask whether to introduce cotton
culture upon a large scale into Africa would be

to secure that African cotton would not be raised by slave labour.

A great deal has been said of the preponderance of population, manufacturing energy, and even agricultural wealth in the North over the South, and we are prepared to admit much; but when it is used as an argument for coercing their neighbours into a change of policy repugnant to their habits, ruinous to their prosperity, and more than doubtful from the experience of other lands, it behoves us to look narrowly into the grounds of such assumed superiority. Hay is one of the great sources of national wealth, which has been prominently put forward as being of more value than all the cotton grown South. Let us look into it.

The object of making hay is to cure the grass so that it can be transported to cover, and feed cattle through those rigorous northern winters, which prevent the cattle from seeking their own food in its natural state. Where those winters do not exist that necessity does not arise, but the cattle have not the less food. The making of hay is then not a valuable labour, but an expense in the keeping of cattle imposed by climate. Accordingly we find, as we proceed south, the winters being shorter, less hay is made in proportion to the number of cattle kept. In Maine, 755,889 tons of hay were made, and there were 385,115 head of cattle and horses to feed. This is a ratio of nearly two tons per head. In Illinois, 601,952 tons of hay were made, but 1,190,264 head of cattle were kept, or rather more than half a ton per head. In Alabama, 32,685 tons of hay were made, and 915,911 head of cattle kept, or about one ton to thirty head of cattle. In the aggregate, the hay crop of the country and the number of cattle kept was as follows:

	No. of Cattle.	Tons hay cut.	lbs. per head.
North . .	5,460,820	9,473,605	3,460
West . .	5,161,895	3,227,253	1,260
South . .	13,475,689	1,137,784	170
Total . .	24,098,404	13,838,642	

This crop of hay, therefore, is a tax upon the labour of the Northern farmer, proportioned to the number of cattle he seeks to winter, and the rigour of the winter he has to provide for. To count this expense among the advantages of free labour is certainly a very fallacious mode of convincing the labourer of its blessings, and would leave the inference that free labour in Maine is much more profitable than in other free States. The advantages of the southern climate are, that not only is natural fodder more abundant, enabling the same land to support more cattle, but the labour which at the North is applied to making that fodder available, is at the South applied to other productions. The labour which at the North will give 100,000,000 lbs. of hay will, at the South, not being needed for that purpose, give 100,000,000 lbs. of cotton, while the cattle are feeding themselves. It is for this, among other reasons, that the aggregate productions of the South are so much more per head than at the North and West. The chief reason is, however, that the labour at the South is collective, while the free labour at the West depends upon its own resources, and is not able to hire the needful help in sowing and harvest seasons. Improvements in machinery have been a great help in that respect, enabling the farmer to get more into, and more off the ground, than his unassisted labour could effect.

Again, the enormous traffic in Southern goods that passes through the hands of traders in the North, all of whom draw a profit *in transitu* can hardly be set against the country which furnishes it as a reason of inferiority. Its action upon the financial dealings of the North is stupendous.

The produce and the bills drawn against foreign shipments form the credits against which the Southern banks draw, and these credits form an important item of deposits in all the Northern banks, but particularly in those of New York City, where the "balance due banks" swells from $17,000,000 to frequently $35,000,000 in the summer, when the crops are mostly realised. The vast movement of produce also gives premiums to the Northern insurance companies, whose swelling dividends and premium shares have been so tempting of late. If the South produces this vast wealth, she does little of her own transportation, banking, insuring, brokerage, but pays liberally on those accounts to the Northern capital employed in those occupations. Those who visit the North in the summer months crowd the hotels and watering-places, and scatter the proceeds of Southern labour broadcast among shopkeepers and tradespeople in return for manufactured articles.

In the last few years of speculative excitement at the West, where such floods of bonds have been sent to New York for negotiation, the presence of the proceeds of Southern crops lying in the New York banks, and by them used to sustain the stock-market, has been a great aid in the negotiation of those Western credits which were applied to the construction of railroads. That large expenditure reflected upon the Western trade, producing an unusual demand for goods, which disappeared when the railroad expenditure ceased. A very considerable portion of the capital created at the South was applied to the consumption of Western produce, since the thousands of men who were employed in building railroads at the West caused a large local demand for that produce on one hand, while they increased the demand for goods on the other. There has, doubtless, been a large amount expended for railroad construction at the South, but this has not been speculative. We shall, in a future chapter, see that although there are as many miles of railroad in operation at the South as at the West, they have cost hardly more than half the money per mile, and their influence in developing local resources has been immense. We shall see that more than 20 per cent. of Western railroad obligations is dishonoured, while none of the Southern roads have failed to pay. The reason is, the superior cheapness of the latter. It is also a peculiar feature of the Southern roads, that their stocks and liabilities are nearly all owned at home. The dividends and interest do not therefore form a drain upon Southern resources; while at the West that drain has reached a very serious extent, and must lead to the breaking up of numerous companies.

The manufactures of the North have not afforded much surplus for export. They were bred up under the protective system, avowedly because they could not compete with the English manufacturer in the market; and it was not to be expected that they could, under such circumstances, do so in a third market. The greatest increase that has taken place in manufactures has been in cotton goods, and these have increased in the proportion in which, as we have seen in a former chapter, the progress of manufactures at the South has occupied the home market. The South afford the material for that manufacture. The exports of breadstuffs and provisions are also due to the South, since but for the quantities of these which are sent North to feed the Eastern States, little or no Western produce could be spared for Europe, even at high prices. In this respect the West is situated like the English West Indies. There is prolific land enough to raise abundance for export, but no labour. The introduction and use of labour-saving machines alone enables the West to export at all. The use of these requires more capital than the agriculturalists generally possess; but with time, no doubt, they will increase.

The West enjoys within its bosom almost limitless supplies of raw material for every description of manufacture except cotton. Its metals, coal, lumber, building materials, raw materials, everything exists in abundance, requiring only capital to develop them rapidly. In this it contrasts strongly with the barren hills of New England, which are as destitute of metals as of fertility. They afford no material for the employment of her busy people, not even a sufficiency of wool. They have hitherto had their food and materials brought to them, and have sent back goods in return, manufactured under cover of those protective tariffs which all consumers have submitted to for their benefit and the convenience of the Federal Union. That state of things cannot last; the West will acquire capital and manufacture for itself. The South is making long strides in the same direction, and all the sooner that the North insists upon manufacturing morality as well as woollens, and filling the South with new principles as well as new shoes.

Sent North.

Bills and raw materials	$262,560,394
Other produce	200,000,000
Total	$462,560,394

Sent South.

Domestic goods	$240,000,000
Imported	106,000,000
Interest, brokerage, &c.	63,200,000
Southern travellers	53,360,394
Total	$462,560,394

This is the vast trade which approximates the sum of the dealings between the North and the South. These transactions influence the earnings, more or less direct, of every Northern man. A portion of every artisan's work is paid for by Southern means. Every carman draws pay, more or less, from the trade of that section : the agents who sell manufactures, the merchants who sell imported goods, the ships that carry them, the builders of the ships, the lumbermen who furnish the material, and all those who supply means of support to them and their families. The brokers, the dealers in Southern produce, the exchange dealers, the bankers, the insurance companies, and all those who are actively employed in receiving and distributing Southern produce, with the long train of persons who furnish them with houses, clothing, supplies, education, religion, amusement, transport, &c., are dependent upon this active interchange, by which at least one thousand millions of dollars come and go between the North and South in a year. The mind can with difficulty contemplate the havoc and misery that must be caused on both sides by the breaking up and sundering of such ties. If we were to penetrate beyond a rupture, and imagine a peaceable separation, by which the North and South should be sundered without hostilities, we might contemplate the condition and prospects of each. From what has been detailed above, as revealed to us from the return of the census, it is quite apparent that the North, as distinguished from the South and West, would be alone permanently injured. Its fortune depends upon manufacturing and shipping; but, as has been seen, it neither raises its own food nor its own raw material, nor does it furnish freights for its own shipping; the South, on the one hand, raises a surplus of food, and supplies the world with raw material. Lumber, hides, cotton, wool, indigo, all that the manufacturer requires, is within its own circle. The requisite capital to put them in action is rapidly accumulating, and in the long run it would lose — after recovering from first disasters — nothing by separation. The North, on the other hand, will have food and raw materials to buy in order to employ its labour; but who will then buy its goods? It cannot supply England; she makes the same things cheaper. The

West will soon be able to supply itself. The South, while having the world as an eager customer for its raw produce, will not want Northern goods; but she will supply with her surplus manufactures the Central and South American countries, as now with her flour. As the world progresses, manufacturing nations will deal less with each other, because they make the same things. Their customers must be tropical and agricultural communities. But if they quarrel with the manners and customs of those countries to the extent of attempting to force upon them a new system or morality, their piety will be its only reward, and the crown of commercial martyrdom may be mistaken for a zany's cap.

Both the South and West have vast natural resources to be developed, and the time for that development is only retarded by the present profits that the North derives from supplying each with those things that they will soon cease to want. The North has no future natural resources. In minerals both the other sections surpass it. In metals it is comparatively destitute; of raw materials it has none. Its ability to feed itself is questionable. Its commerce is to the whole country what that of Holland once was to the whole world, viz., living on the trade of other people. Its manufactures occupy the same position, awaiting only the time when the other sections will do their own work. When that moment arrives, Massachusetts, which now occupies the proudest rank in the Union, will fall back on her own resources, and still claim to be an agricultural State, since her summer crop is granite and her winter crop is ice. This period the North supinely permits a few unscrupulous politicians, clerical agitators, and reprobate parsons to hasten, by the most wanton attacks upon the institutions of their best customers. They are forcing the Northern slave States to assume to the South the same position that New England held to the South on the formation of the Union. They are holding out to them the bright prize of becoming the manufacturers, importers, and carriers for the South, as the North has been. They offer them this brilliant premium to cut their connection with the North, in order to enjoy those branches of industry in relation to the South which have conferred such wealth and prosperity upon New England and the middle States. England became richer by the colonies,—repelled them. Her mantle fell on the New England States. They have become rich; and in their turn repel the South in favour of the Northern slave States. These latter see the prize falling to them, and may become eager to grasp it before the North shall have awakened to its danger.

Then, again, as to the carrying trade exclusively enjoyed by the North, which surely cannot be claimed as a matter of superiority:—

	Enrolled and Registered.	Cotton Bales.		Enrolled and Registered.	Cotton Bales.
1820	1,119,736	225,000	1849	2,527,972	2.728,596
1830	990,260	976,845	1850	2,609,544	2.006,706
1835	1,580,481	1,254,328	1851	2,753,182	2,355.257
1840	1,709,318	2,177,885	1852	3,070,431	3,015,029
1841	1,691,092	1,634.945	1853	3,388,637	3,262,892
1842	1,612,950	1,638,574	1854	3,747.212	2,930,027
1843	1.668,271	2,378,875	1855	4,059.162	2,847,339
1844	1,707,160	2,030,409	1856	3,841,047	3,527,845
1845	1,769,387	2,394,503	1857	3,862,812	2,939,519
1846	1,885,284	2,100,537	1858	3,933,453	3,113,962
1847	2,095,236	1,778,651	1859	3,977,970	3,851,481
1848	2,261,804	2,347,634	1860	4,000,000	4,300,000

The sailing vessels under the head of enrolled are to a considerable extent engaged in the transport of cotton. As a general rule a registered ton will carry three bales. A great deal of cotton is subject, however, to several distinct transports. It is delivered at the South ports by steam and other boats, thence sent to North ports to be shipped to England or to manufacturing towns. This movement so governs the shipping trade, that whenever the quantity has been stimulated beyond one ton to a bale produced in the aggregate, there has been invariably reaction and depression. In 1820 the shipping was large because there existed remains of the trade during the French wars, and the tonnage lost, condemned and sold had not then been fully marked off from the official registers. Since then the account has been accurately kept. The quantity built was small up to 1830, when the proportion of one ton to a bale existed. From 1835, when the same proportion was apparent, there was little variation in the quantity built per annum, and the proportions of shipping to cotton held good up to the large crop of 1843, which immediately gave an impulse to the business of shipbuilding; and tonnage increased annually up to 1846, when the amount had again reached the proportion of one ton to a bale. In that year, however, took place the Irish famine, causing a demand for ships all over the world for transport of grain. This demand was aided by the Mexican war, for which Government required much transport service. The shipbuilding reached 3,318,075 tons in 1848, in which year those two elements had ceased to act, and there was a heavy depression in the trade since the tonnage exceeded the proportion of one ton to a bale. In 1850 and 1851 and in 1852 the proportion was recovered, but then took place the revolution in shipbuilding, caused by California. Clipper ships became the rage, and the gold trade carried the tonnage far beyond the regular cotton proportion. The result was the same as before. A terrible depression overtook shipping, and building, which had been carried to its greatest height in 1855, when it reached 2034 vessels, with a tonnage of 583,450, has year by year declined; the quantity lost, condemned, and sold to foreigners has been more than equal to the production, and the sale tonnage is now 91,192 tons less than at the highest point in 1855. The cotton crop has, however, increased, until it has resumed its proportion of one bale to a ton. There can be no clearer proof than these figures afford, of the utter dependence of the North shipping on the great South staple. If we turn to the official tables distinguishing the three sections, we shall have the ownership of tonnage as follows, comparing the years 1830 and 1858, both cotton crop and tonnage having quadrupled :—

	1830.			1858.		
	Registered.	Enrolled.		Registered.	Enrolled.	
		Sail.	Steam.		Sail.	Steam.
South .	109,182	82,849	33,605	391,518	297,394	229,180
West .	54	2,090	219	50,236	219,416	104,009
North .	380,826	471,682	20,010	1,781,369	1,381,893	318,174
Total .	490,062	556,621	54,036	2,223,123	1,898,693	651,363

	Registered Tons.	Value Shipping.	Extent of Freight.
North . . .	1,781,368	73,145,879	2,000,000
South . . .	391,518	17,618,111	24,500,000
West . . .	50,236	2,260,620	1,500,000
Total . .	2,223,132	93,024,610	28,000,000

The South furnishes six-sevenths of the freight,
but owns less than one-sixth of the tonnage. The
North owns eighty per cent. of tonnage, and supplies seven per cent. of freights. The value is given
much less than actual amount; thus the cotton crop
of the present year will reach 2,070,000,000 lbs.,
and the present rate of freight is one cent per lb.,
or ten per cent. of the value. This gives nearly
21,000,000 freights for one transport of the crop,
and it requires several. The other articles of export
bear a similar freight of the registered tonnage at
the North. New York City holds half of the outward freights from there. A large portion of that
put down to the West is supplanted by South produce received coastwise, and it is not otherwise to
be spared from North consumption. These are the
outward freights only. The return freights into
the country are also to a considerable extent on

South account, at the same rate per cent., on the value as that paid by cotton. The amount derived on the importations is $35,000,000 per annum, of which *pro ratâ* $12,000,000 is paid by South consumers. We have then $36,000,000 paid by South to the shipping per annum, or a sum double the value of all the tonnage she owns, and this without taking into account in any degree the coasting freights. This large sum is distributed among the merchants, owners, seamen, shipbuilders, stevedores, carmen, and all their business connections, as the value of the South connection. That section consents to the profits thus enjoyed by the North, while she has it in her power to withdraw them by a resort to her own forests and shipyards. The North thus monopolises the freights, for the reason that she has hitherto been able to furnish the cheapest ships. The South has, no doubt, however, profited by the cheap freights. Had the two sections not been united by the bond of free trade, a very little legislation would have caused shipbuilding to grow faster at the South than it has hitherto. The evils of disunion would be not unconnected with some benefit for the Maryland and Delaware shipbuilders in this respect. The coasting tonnage is supported in nearly the same manner as the registered tonnage, and it is the North that draws the benefit.

Let us turn to another point of view, in estimating the commercial value of the two sections relatively to each other, viz. railroads, more especially interesting in the country which owes its physical power and position mainly to their development. The account stands somewhat thus:—

If the South has not built as much tonnage as it required for its business, allowing the North to carry its produce, it has not been behind in the building of railroads. It has built them, however, with its own capital. The effect of this large construction at the South, was to absorb the capital which, earned by cotton, had of late accumulated, and prevent it from going more into manufacturing. It will be observed that the South built more miles of rail in the six years to 1860, than did the West; but they did not exhaust their means in so doing. The West is prostrate under the effort, while the South was never more solid. It has now before it the roads to assist in an active development of other interests of the cotton proceeds.

The sugar, cotton, and tobacco, finds its way to a considerable extent across the country into the West States, and these roads have been built in the West section to a very large proportion with borrowed money. They have consequently been built expensively; far more so than those of the South. The aggregate length and cost of railroads has been as follows: —

	1853.		1860.		
	Length.	Cost.	Length.	Cost.	Per Mile.
		$		$	$
North . .	7,222	287,691,587	9,665	481,874,434	50,000
West . .	5,535	110,389,337	9,191	365,109,701	40,000
South . .	4,663	91,522,204	9,053	221,857,503	24,100
Total .	17,420	489,603,128	27,909	1,068,841,638	

These returns for 1853 are from the census returns, and for 1860 are from the "Boston Railway Times," compiled by an eminent engineer. We have then the fact that the South has as many miles of railroad as either of the other sections, and that they cost per mile less than half the cost of the North roads, and two-thirds the expense of the West, a fact which shows the economy with which the South roads were built. We now take from "Stone's Railway Annual" the roads delinquent on interest of bond: —

	Companies.	Amount.
South	3	$2,025,000
North	9	39,000,000
West	21	68,120,000
Total . .	33	$109,215,000

The business of the South has, it appears, paid the cost of 9053 miles of road, when the North has been unable to do so; and the West has shown still less ability to sustain that length of road. The capital supplied to the latter section for construction came from England and the East States, and was expended in a lavish manner, stimulating business and speculation, which has fallen through, leaving a disastrous condition of affairs in all that region. The roads themselves show in the declining revenues the fact that they owed their former prosperity less to the effects of free labour than to the factitious activity caused by a passing speculation. The crops of that region are not like those of the South, in constant and active demand, pressing always by the shortest road to market; they depend for realisation on short crops abroad. In ordinary seasons the price will not pay for transport by rail, while the South becomes an active competitor with the West for the supply of the North and East States by water.

The rapid circulation of the commercial value thus tells upon the banks at New York, which absorb largely the profits of the Southern trade:—

The concentration of capital at New York promotes its own development, or " makes the meat it feeds on." The manufacturers of Europe and of the East, and the agriculturists of the West and the South, all send their capital to New York on credit, and, singularly enough, to obtain credit. All Europe contributes to her apparent capital, and swells the deposits in her banks. The process is a very simple one. The European manufacturer ships to a New York factor dry goods, consisting of silks, laces, &c.; he is apprised that long credits must be given to insure a sale of these goods, say eight to twelve months from day of sale. The factor disposes of these goods to the jobber, taking his paper in settlement. This paper is generally at once placed on the market, and sold at market rates for money. Thus the factor is at once supplied with money, belonging, in fact, to his European correspondent, which he can use in any way he thinks proper, only taking care to be able to transmit money to Europe at the time that the notes taken for the goods fall due. The wholesale jobber repeats the same operation in his sale in like manner to the wholesale and retail merchant. Their paper is at once turned into cash, giving to the jobber great appearance of strength at his bank, and also a large cash capital, to be invested in stocks, or shaving paper, or any other manner fancy or judgment may dictate. The wholesale merchant sells in like manner to country merchants, whose paper is also thrown upon the market, where it is saleable. Thus the same article, sold successively on time, furnishes the appearance of real capital to several different merchants. The same operation is repeated in the sale of the various other articles imported from Europe to this country. In like manner the manufacturers of New England furnish capital to New York. They consign their manufactures to a New York agent, and have a time draft on him discounted at their own banks. If the agent succeeds in selling the goods promptly, he has the use of the money till the maturity of the draft. Again, the money to buy this paper is not by any means contributed alone by New York capitalists. Some of the banks of South Carolina are charged with buying up the paper of Southern men through their agents in New York. Large amounts of capital are known to be sent on from Virginia and other parts of the South for the same purpose.

With the Southern banks, a preference is given to a four months' note on personal security. The manufacturers of tobacco are compelled, in order to raise money to carry on their business in Virginia, to have a Northern correspondent, upon whom they draw these bills, and to whom their tobacco must be consigned. As the bills are drawn on the consignment of tobacco, that must go forward, no matter what is the state of the market in New York, and no matter how much depressed the article may be by reason of want of demand, or a glut in the market.

When the tobacco arrives in New York, the agent there sells the tobacco as soon as he thinks proper, generally for an eight months' note. He immediately takes the note, places it in the hands of a broker, who sells it at the current rates for similar paper. The proceeds, less the commission and a share, are returned to the agent, who uses it in paying other acceptances falling due, it may be to other parties, or he applies the money to purposes of private speculation, thus being supplied with capital by the Virginia banks. The value of the manufactured tobacco is estimated at $15,000,000.

A planter in the South cannot borrow money from the bank upon a pledge of his land and negroes, or on good personal security, or even upon a promise to turn over to the bank the proceeds of his crop when sold. He can, however, borrow, by drawing on his factor, who sells his cotton. These drafts, from the nature of the case, fall due during the early part of the crop year. In like manner, the shipper of cotton to England cannot obtain money except by drawing a sterling bill, which is a bill payable sixty days after sight. Formerly, an advance to a planter really meant what it purports to be. Now an advance consists in the acceptance of a draft, and if the planter's cotton is not in time to protect it, long and loud are the complaints against the dishonesty of planters in withholding their crops to meet their just debts. It is easy to see how this mode of banking affects the price of cotton, and depresses it beyond its true value. No one expects to obtain anything like full value from a sale by a pawnbroker of a watch pledged for a debt, even in prosperous times. Of course, when times are bad, the sacrifice is much greater. But the Southern people have made the movement of the sale of cotton dependent, in a great degree, upon the condition of affairs in New York, caused either by their want of ability, or willingness, to pay their debts to Europe; then the Southern banks cannot buy sterling bills, and the shipper cannot buy cotton. Even when cotton is bought and shipped, either to New York or Europe, it becomes completely in the power of the buyers to control the price of cotton. The banks, refusing to give the acceptor of the bills any accommodation, necessitates

the sale of the articles pledged on arrival to meet
the bill at maturity. However honest he may be
and anxious to promote the interest of the consig-
nor, necessity having no law, he is compelled to sell
at prices dictated by the buyer.

The capital of all sections, in all shapes, is thus
poured into New York through the hands of the
bankers, and becomes the means of floating a large
amount of securities of all description. The Southern
produce which comes there pays a large profit to agents
of all kinds, through whose hands it passes, and the
goods which come there are, to a large amount, sold
to the South on credit, on which Southern money
lying in New York is advanced, to be used in such
purposes of speculation as frequently bring on a
panic, and depress the price of both bills and cotton.
The summer is the season when the largest supply
of Southern funds becomes apparent, and it is then
the banks are most anxious to make it draw interest.
They lend it upon stocks, and cause an inflation by
speculators, who bid high for money. In the fall,
when those funds are again wanted for their legitimate purposes, they cannot be recalled from speculation so readily, and the notes of the mercantile
people are thrown out rather than that the paying

loans to the speculators should be disturbed. The pretence is that specie is going abroad, and that it is the importers who send it. Their paper is consequently thrown out, preventing them from buying bills. By the same operation the price of cotton is depressed. Thus at the same time the value of bills drawn against cotton is depressed at the same moment that the price of the article itself falls.

The produce of the country is shipped and drawn against supplying, in round numbers, $350,000,000 of exchange. Nearly the whole of this amount is sold to banks and bankers, who hold it as a sort of monopoly, awaiting the demands of merchants who, having imported $330,000,000 worth of goods, must pay for them. There are also $20,000,000 to be remitted for interest on debts, public and corporate, and probably $30,000,000 more as the expenses of Americans travelling abroad. Now the only mode for making these remittances is to buy bills, and the remitters must pay the price asked. In all the cities of Europe there is a variety of counter-exchange, by which the merchant may arbitrate his remittances as he pleases. If in Paris he wants to remit to London, he may buy a bill on London, or may order his creditors in London to draw on him ; or he may buy a bill on any other city, to remit or order a draft on any other city to be sold. Twenty combinations may be calculated, and the cheapest acted upon. The American merchant has but one choice. He may give the banker his price for a bill or remit the coin himself. The effect of this monopoly of the exchange market by the banker, aids the concentration of money in New York, and in a similar manner the internal exchanges are more or less controlled. The rate is always at a premium in New York, and that frequently when New York is in debt, the real rate of exchange being disguised in depreciation of local currency. The Southern banks having large deposits in New York drawing interest, do not sell exchange against those funds, but in some cases buy commercial exchange for depreciated notes, and then supply the market only as it will bear a premium. If their funds did not draw interest at the North, and their own paper was payable on demand, actually as well as nominally, the exchange rate would be as often below as above par. At bottom, the same system exists as with the external exchange, viz., always to draw, and never to be drawn upon.

Exports, domestic produce .	.	.	$278,392,080
Surplus, California gold product	.	.	42,000,000
Freight earnings, estimate .	.	.	30,000,000
Total to credit .	.	.	350,392,080
Interest due abroad .	. $15,000,000		
Expenses of travellers .	. 20,000,000		
			35,000,000
			315,392,080
Actual net imports, 1859	.	.	316,823,370

This gives the amount of goods that are received in exchange for produce sold. It is obvious that unless the produce is given away something must be taken in' payment. As they produce gold in sums larger than the country requires, that cannot be imported to advantage. They have food and raw material in excess, and can therefore, if they trade at all, take only such foreign wares as those who buy of them can supply to the best advantage. The food, the gold, and the cotton they sell Europe must have, and sales of these regulate the quantities of goods pretty nearly that come back. The kind of goods so received depend in some degree on their ability to compete with the Northern manufacturers who have the preference. If Massachusetts factories can make a certain style of cotton goods as cheap as the English — it has a duty of 20 per cent. and 10 per cent. charges or 30 per cent. preference over the

English, which ensures it the market at a large profit, the account is sometimes disturbed by credit, as in the case of the recent railroad speculation. Large sums are sent from England there for investment; if these in one year reach, say $30,000,000, goods to that amount may be and are imported in addition. It also happens at such seasons that sellers supply goods on credit to other than regular merchants. Those dealers sustain themselves by bank operations, until explosion takes place ; the trade then settles back to the real staple exports of the country, and these are of Southern origin. The leading exports from time to time have been as follows :—

Year.	Cotton.	Tobacco.	Flour and Provisions.	Rice.	Manufactures.
	$	$	$	$	$
1790	42,285	4,349,567	5,991,171	1,753,796	
1803	7,920,000	6,209,000	15,050,000	2,455,000	2,000.000
1807	14,232,000	5,476.000	15,706,000	2,307,000	2,309,000
1816	24,106.000	12,809,000	29,587,376	2,378,880	2,331.000
1821	20,157,484	5,648.962	12,341,360	1,494,387	2,752,631
1831	31,724,682	4.892.388	12,424,701	2,016,267	5.086,890
1836	71,284,925	10,058,640	9,588,359	2.548,750	6,107,528
1842	47,693,464	9,540,755	16,902,876	1,907,387	7,102,101
1847	53,415.808	7,242.086	68,701,921	3,605,896	10,351,364
1851	112,315,717	9,219.251	21,948,651	2,170,997	20,136,967
1859	161,434,923	21,074,018	37,987,395	2,207,148	32,471,927

The New England States, which are so largely manufacturing, do not, with the exception of a small quantity of wool, produce any of the raw materials which they require, nor do they produce coal, or iron, or wheat. The census of 1850 shows that the value of their agricultural products is only $15 per head of the population, a quantity unequal to the support of life. An able writer in Boston states that in 1858 one-third of all the flour and five-sevenths of all the corn sold in Boston was received from the commercial ports of the Southern States. In addition to the great staple articles, cotton, tobacco, and sugar, the Southern States send North vast quantities of Indian corn, rice, sweet potatoes, hemp, naval stores, timber, wool, flour, wheat, live-stock, and various other products.

The Census of 1850 gives the number of live-stock
   in the Southern States at that time   .   .   . $40,823,727
In the Northern States   36,409,134

But these matters are more for the American citizens themselves than for us. The main question for us to look at is, what has been the cause of this disunion, and who is to blame?

CHAP. IV.

A GREAT writer has published his views lately on the question with a bias which has led him into fallacy. Mr. Motley tells us " that as long as efforts had been confined to argument, it was considered sufficient to answer the argument, but now that secession, instead of remaining a topic of vehement and subtle discussion, has expanded into armed and fierce rebellion and revolution, civil war is the inevitable result." Of course it is; but the responsibility lies at the door of those who by a systematic and violent series of attacks on the property and even the lives of their fellow-citizens, forced them into an attitude of defence. The armed and fierce action was entirely on the part of the North. They appeal to arms, and on them lies the heavy onus. Moreover, I have shown above that the whole has been done on their side by the President alone, as Dictator, without any legal or constitutional action of the people by their representatives. Mr. Motley allows " the fabric of American empire ought to rest on the solid basis of the consent of the people." When has the consent of the people been taken on this issue ? He allows, " the right of revolution exists indisputably the sole arbiter being the tribunal of the civilised world and future ages." What has barred the Southern States from this dread appeal? Has one drop of blood been shed on Northern soil ? Was not the armed invasion of the Southern States a direct appeal to the God of battles, which men, fighting for their lives, their homes, and property, were bound to take up as they have done, manfully, fearlessly and with a declaration of their rights, and a determination to assert them before the face of day. Unless a two-thirds vote in both Houses of Congress and a ratification in three-fourths of the whole number of States make the law of the land binding on every subject, the action of the President is as lawless as it is sanguinary. History will decide whether the resistance is " rebellion, treason, plunder," and we do not fear her verdict. When he says that " the secession of the South, followed by the destruction of the whole body politic of which they were vital parts, was in contempt of any other remedy for *expected* grievances," no man knows better than Mr. Motley the utter worthlessness of such assertion. "Expected grievances" indeed! He knows what vital interests were menaced, what attacks had been made and were preparing against them. It is certainly true, as Judge Story lays it down, that in the General Convention of 1787 there was no reservation of any right on the part of any state to dissolve its connection, or to abrogate its dissent, or to suspend the operation of the constitution as to itself; but the language of Virginia was explicit. " The powers granted under the constitution, being derived from the people of the United States, may be resumed by them whenever the same shall be perverted to their injury and oppression." There are times and there are occasions, when, in self-defence and in self-preservation, men appeal to higher laws than are to be found in the statute book, and the Southern States affirm that such a time has come, such an occasion has arisen, and they may be sure Englishmen are the last people in the civilised world to deny their appeal. They know that the oft-repeated assertion, " that the Republican party, in determining to set bounds to the extension of slavery, had no designs, secret or avowed, against slavery within the States," is a patent, palpable, and wicked lie; and " the noble and generous desire of all parties in the Free

States to vindicate the sullied honour of their flag" is mere bunkum, to get him the loaves and fishes which we see Mr. Motley has posted off to Washington to secure.

Let us now turn to a far different controversialist, Mr. Helper, the author of the " Land of Gold," and the refugee from Raleigh, North Carolina, under circumstances which he would do well to atone by repaying his employer, the bookseller, the 300 dollars of his he took by mistake. This gentleman's appeal to civilised nations runs thus: " Too long have we yielded a submissive obedience to the tyrannical domination of an inflated oligarchy, too long have we tolerated their arrogance and self-conceit, their unjust and savage exactions. Let us now wrest from them the sceptre of power, and establish liberty and equal rights throughout the land." Brave words, Mr. Helper ! His oligarchy are the " knights of the whip and the lash," " haughty cavaliers of shackles and handcuffs," whose " demagogical manœuvrings," "tricks of legerdemain," "nonsensical ravings," " incoherent and truth-murdering declamations," are " basely duping, adroitly swindling, and damnably outraging the poor," " so that the South, wofully inert and inventionless, has lagged behind the North, and lies weltering in the cesspool of ignorance and degradation," he evidences by recounting a long list of Presidents, Vice-Presidents, Judges of the Supreme Court, Secretaries of State, Speakers of the House of Representatives, Attorney-Generals, and other dignitaries, under whose beneficent and judicious rule the United States has achieved the marvellous greatness of her empire. These gentlemen, in a most Christian spirit, he proposes, " as a reasonable expiation for the countless evils which they have inflicted on society, to clothe themselves in sackcloth, and, after a suitable season of contrition and severe penance, follow the example of one Judas Iscariot, and go and hang themselves." We might afford to leave Mr. Helper to the indignation and scorn of those unfortunate enough to be compelled to read 413 pages of such a work, but there are others in high places and seemingly honoured in the North, who not only indorse this Helper's views, but have recorded their approbation in solemn language before the Houses of Assembly and before the face of Europe. William Lloyd Garrison proposed on July 4th, 1856, " to register a pledge before heaven to do what within him lay to effect the eternal overthrow of the blood-stained Union." Horace Greely, " better that the capital itself should blaze by the torch of the incendiary, or fall and bury all beneath its crumbling ruins, than to cease from agitation." Is this the spirit, Mr. Greely, in which you propose to carry on the *Tribune*, of which you are the Government organ? in the way which, last month, you proposed the simultaneous attack on Canada by a United North and South? Joshua R. Giddings "looked forward to the day when the torch of the incendiary shall light up the towns and cities of the South, which he should hail as the dawn of a political millennium." These, Mr. Giddings, are the "expected grievances" for which, we presume, your friend Mr. Motley suggests other remedies. N. P. Banks, now Major-General of the Federal army, Speaker of the House of Representatives, and late Governor of Massachusetts, is willing "to let the Union slide." Rufus B. Spaulding "is for dissolution, and cares not how soon it comes." Horace Mann is "for abolition, if it should send all the party organisations in the Union, or the Union itself, to the devil." Erastus Hopkins, "where ballots are useless would make ballots effective;" and General Watson Webb, now Minister to Brazil, in the convention that nominated Fremont for the Presidency, amid tremendous applause propounded, "that republicans should force back the slaveocracy with fire and the sword." Such sentiments from such men need no comment from me.

The latest writer on this question is Thomas Ellison, of whose views and calm serenity of style the following pasage is a fair specimen:—

" Every attempt to restore peace to the Union by means of congressional action failed. The treasonable, high-handed, and most unreasonable attitude of the secession disgusted every moderate and sensible man in Congress, and consequently the majority in both Houses were indisposed to conciliation, or anything akin to it.*　The South will receive a wholesome lesson in civilised morality, in the shape of thorough castigation.　It may bluster and threaten and fume, but its paroxysms would only add to its own suffering—it will sink into almost unfathomable debt, and lose the sympathy of all Christendom, except as a repentant."　Kind prophecy this, but not borne out as yet.　Again, " Mr. Davis's Message was a mere rehash of what was said before.　It is remarkable more for what it does not than for what it does say.　It ignores the real cause of the crisis, and endeavours to throw all the blame on the shoulders of the Federal Government, whereas, if the Government has sinned at all, it has been in being

* But they seized the occasion to pass the Protectionist Morill Tariff !

too lenient to the Southern conspirators." "Lincoln, from the very first, acted purely on the defensive; Davis, on the aggressive. Federal property was plundered and destroyed to an enormous extent, the Government flag insulted on every available occasion, Washington threatened with bombardment, and many people coerced into submission by the demagogues. Clearly the war was originated by the South, and on their heads must fall the consequences of their evil doings." Is this an impartial summing up of facts, or a foregone conclusion?

Again, " There is no doubt that justice and right are on the side of the North. The South has refused to accept all constitutional remedies for its real or supposed grievances" (we had this before from Mr. Motley), " and preferred to hew itself out of the Union amid blood and carnage of civil war. There was no need for the sword! The slave-owners have refused to allow their own people to vote on the adoption of their constitution. They are rebels, and even if they succeed in establishing their separate existence, the civil war they have inaugurated will ever remain a foul blot upon their fame."*

But as he adduces certain reasons for the action

---

* Ellison, p. 140.

of the Federal Government, it will be well to see what they are worth. His position is this :—

" It became clear (A.D. 1820) to the leaders of both parties that some halfway measure would be the only method of settling the dispute; hence the support which welcomed the celebrated Amendment of Mr. Thomas, since known as the Missouri Compromise : the closing votes were :—Senate—yeas, 90 ; nays, 87.* House—yeas, 134 ; nays, 42. ' And be it further enacted that in all the territory ceded by France to the United States, under the name of Louisiana, which lies N. 36° 30', not included within the limits of the State contemplated by this Act, slavery and involuntary servitude, otherwise than in the punishment of crimes whereof the parties shall have been duly convicted, shall be and is hereby for ever prohibited. Provided always, that any person escaping into the same from whom labour or service is lawfully claimed in any State or terri-tory of the United States, such fugitive may be lawfully reclaimed and conveyed to the person claiming his or her labour or service aforesaid.' "†

" The South is strictly an agricultural country, and under slavery can never be anything else. Hence

* How can Mr. Ellison make these numbers ?
† Ellison, p. 21.

her commercial interests would be best forwarded by an entire freedom of trade with the manufacturing world. But the North is a manufacturing community, and requires a protective tariff in order to enable it to compete with the cheap fabrics of Europe. The South grumbles, but requiring the aid of at least some Northern votes, to secure the integrity of the "domestic institution," Southern slaveholding Whigs have always exchanged votes with Northern Protectionist Whigs, so that a United North with but little Southern help could keep down the free-trade predilections of the South, and a United South with but a little Northern aid could keep in abeyance Northern anti-slavery measures. So the interdependence was secured: the North supplying grain, animals, machinery, and manufactures to the South; and the South raw cotton, minerals, sugar, and rice to the North. The connection was nearly broken in 1832 by the disaffection of the South; they had often expressed themselves strongly, but were always overwhelmed by the Northern *interest.*"*

"The Northern manufacturers claimed that the revenue should be levied in such a way as to protect their productions against the competition of

* Ellison, p. 26.

European fabrics. Their request was granted. The same principle was acted upon in all subsequent revisions of the tariff, but the opposition of the South, at first feeble, gained strength as time grew, till in 1831, when the National Debt was nearly paid off and the revenue considerably exceeded the expenditure, the South made a decided stand, and demanded reductions of tariff." *

" In 1850, discussions on the organisation of the new territories in Mexico and Utah were renewed. Things assumed an awkward aspect; the Free Soilers were strong and determined, and their opponents equally so; the issue would doubtless have been serious had not the ingenuity of Clay bolstered and only bolstered matters by a new compromise. In this measure several old disputes were settled. Clay's proposition was that the territories should be organised on ' squatter sovereignty,' i. e. the settlers choose their own constitution. This was the concession of the South. On their part the Free States accepted the Fugitive Slave Clause. Constitutionally the slave-owners had held this right from 1787, but their attempts at reclamation had always been frustrated." †

" The Kansas Nebraska Act expressly declares

<hr>

* Ellison, p. 29.   † Ibid. p. 32.

the Missouri Compromise 'inoperative and void.' Down to 1854 the compact had been kept inviolate, the Mexico and Utah measures being below the compromise line. The admission of Missouri and Arkansas was one of the conditions of the compromise, and the framers never dreamt that the territories north of the line would be interfered with. The North had all along been too conciliatory, too faithful to the South; but when the slave-owners had secured the whole territory south of the line, they repudiated the compromise, and declared it unconstitutional for Congress to interfere with the constitutional organisation of the territories, and cut their northern tools." *

The consequence of which he candidly puts into the mouth of Mr. Wade, who, in a speech at Washington, announced the programme of what he has since carried out with the rest of his party (see p. 5). He then goes through the events immediately preceding the secession, commenting on President Buchanan's message to Congress, thus:—

" Such a feeble, vacillating, inconsistent, pusillanimous, and glaringly partisan document was never delivered from the White House. A perusal left

* Ellison, p. 34.

the impression on our mind that the whole was an elaborate defence of the South, and we were led to believe so irresolute and contradictory a document could not have been the production of one mind or of a United Cabinet. There is every reason to believe Buchanan had been compelled by the pro-secession portion to append his signature to a meaningless and unintelligible concourse of words." *

He quotes Wade :—

" Like a spoilt child, the South must have all it demands. The twenty millions of free men must submit to the wilfulness of about half a million of slaveholders. The Republican party must give up its victory, and quietly and submissively submit to the yoke of slavedom. During the past twenty-five years the South has been the victim of Northern virulence, the hunted lambs of Northern wolves." †

" Attorney-General Black, in Nov. 1860, defined the relations between the States and the Federal Government : 'The will of a State, whether expressed in its constitution or laws, cannot, while it remains in the confederacy, absolve her people from the duty of obeying the just and constitutional requirements of the central government. Nor can

* Ellison, p. 72.   † Ibid. p. 73.

any act of the central government displace the jurisdiction of a State, because the laws of the United States are supreme and binding only so far as they are passed in pursuance of the constitution. I do not say what might be effected by mere revolutionary force; I am speaking of legal and constitutional right.'

" Judge Wade, of Ohio, p. 80, said, 'I acknowledge to the fullest extent the right of revolution, if you so call it, a right to destroy the Government, and erect another on its ruins more in accordance with your wishes. But when you undertake it, it is with this provision : if you are successful, all is right —you are heroes; but if you are defeated, you are rebels. This is the character of revolutions. If successful, all well; if not, the Government treats them as traitors.'"*

And also Mr. Douglas :—

" Doubtless the United North could subdue the United South if it willed to do so, but it could not be expected that the defeated States would be reconciled to the Union by such means. They would give a kind of allegiance to the Federal power, but under protest, and therefore but transient. They would have no love to the Union, and would take the

* Ellison, p. 78.　　　　† Ibid. p. 80.

earliest favourable opportunity of breaking it up. Their pride, wounded by defeat, would never let them rest until they had achieved their independence. If, therefore, the Union cannot be preserved by peaceful means, by mutual concessions, if the same influences which called it into being, mutual interests and reciprocal affections, no longer exist, the confederacy had better be peaceably dissolved."*

Douglas, January 3rd, 1861, said : —

" There is no other resource left to enforce the law in a seceding State, except to make war and bring the State into possession first. A war between eighteen States on one side, and fifteen seceding States on the other, is a revolting thing. And for what purpose is it waged? certainly not for the purpose of preserving the Union. You cannot expect to exterminate ten millions of people whose passions are excited with the belief that you mean to invade their homes and light the flames of insurrection in their midst. Sooner or later both parties will become exhausted, and when rendered incapable of fighting any longer they will make a peace—but of separation. The history of the world does not furnish an example of a war of sections

* Ellison, p. 83.

or states of the same nation which ended in reconciliation. Where there is a deep-seated discontent
pervading ten millions, penetrating every man,
woman, and child, involving everything dear to
them, it is time to inquire whether there is not a
cause." *

And Mr. Iverson :—

" If you acknowledge our independence and treat
us as one of the nations of the earth, you can have
friendly relations and intercourse, you can have an
equitable division of public property and the existing public debt of U. S. ; but if you make war
upon us, we will seize and hold all the public property in our borders, and we will never pay one
dollar of the public debt. The first Federal gun
that is fired on the seceding States, the first drop of
blood of any of our people shed by the Federal troops,
will cancel every debt, public and private, to the
Federal Government or Northern people. We care
not in what shape or form you attempt coercion.
We consider all acts to enforce authority over us
war, and meet and resist accordingly. And fighting on our own soil, and to preserve our rights,
vindicate our honour, defend our homes, our fire-

* Ellison, p. 85.

sides, wives and children from the invader, we shall not easily be conquered. You may possibly overrun and desolate our fields, lay our cities in ruins, murder our people, and reduce us to beggary, but you cannot subdue or subjugate us to your will: you would have to keep a standing army of 100,000 men, costing millions, only to keep us under. We will rise again and again to vindicate our rights and liberties, and throw off your oppressive and accursed yoke, and never cease the strife till our whole race is extinguished. You may blockade our ports, and lock up our commerce: but we shall see what other nations will say. I know hopes are raised and great efforts made to retain the Border States in the Union; but the first gun fired, the first ship stationed off our ports, will bring all the States, including Maryland, laggard as she seems to be in the vindication of sound independence, into obedience and alliance with her Southern sisters, and thus united they will resist and defy all your efforts." *

On the other hand he reviews the reasons for secession, and the grievances complained of, thus:—

" Whatever loss South Carolina suffered from non-reddition of slaves from Free States, there was a con-

* Mr. Iverson, January 28th, in the Senate.

stitutional remedy. The law, if properly carried out, will ensure the return, any enactments of the separate States to the contrary notwithstanding. If some of the Free States have, *as asserted*, made laws which nullify Acts of Congress, or render useless an attempt to execute them, the proper remedy is for Congress to assert its dignity and demand the repeal of such laws. A little quiet remonstrance on the part of Government would soon settle it. But it is questionable whether South Carolina ever experienced the loss of more than one or two runaways since the Union. South Carolina's complaint, therefore, is unfounded and extremely frivolous.

" But the slaveholders are conscious that during their long tenure of office they behaved in the most intolerant manner towards the Free States ; had bullied them into compromise and then repudiated and maltreated their citizens, and attempted to deprive them of constitutional rights, and naturally expected the time had come when the South was to be punished for its offences. But here the constitution would have preserved them ; for before slavery can be touched the constitution must be amended, and that can only be done with the consent of three-fourths of the whole number of States. It will be seen then how idle are the fears of South

Carolina on account of republican hostility to negro bondage. Her plea is most puerile. How much better and more manly to have waited till the President gave the world a declaration of his principles and intentions; she would then have received the sympathy of all impartial men on both sides of the Atlantic. As it is, the proceedings are by many looked on as farcical. The declarations are read sometimes in ironical, sometimes in serio-comic tones; some pity, others contemn. The majority say, let her alone; experience will show the folly of her doings. The muscular majority suggest she get a sound thrashing. All are disgusted."*

But the history of proceedings goes on to show:—

" A copy of the ordinance of secession was laid before the President of the United States, with the request it should be communicated to Congress, then in session, and to treat for the delivery of forts, magazines, and light-houses, and other real estate and appurtenances thereto, within the geographical limits of South Carolina ; for an apportionment of the public debt and a division of all other property held by the government of the United States, as agent of the Confederated States, of which South Carolina was

* Ellison, p. 90.

recently a member, and generally to negotiate as to all other measures and arrangements proper to be made and adopted in the existing relation of the parties, and for the continuance of peace and amity between that commonwealth and the government at Washington. R. W. Barnwell, J. H. Adams, and James L. Orr, as commissioners, announced to President Lincoln, December 29, 1860, that South Carolina resumed the powers she delegated to the United States, and declared her perfect sovereignty and independence; they were prepared to enter into negotiations with the earnest desire to avoid hostilities and inaugurate new relations, so as to secure mutual respect, general advantage, and future goodwill and harmony. Buchanan acknowledged 'that Major Anderson had somewhat exceeded his orders, which were to make no movement until he was attacked,' and stated, 'that when he learned that the Major had removed from Fort Moultrie to Sumpter, his first impulse was to order him to retrace his steps and await further orders;' but hostilities had then begun. The commissioners replied 'that they had no solicitude as to the character in which they might be recognised, being satisfied of the unquestionable right of their State to act as they had done, and declared they were ready for war if he chose to force that issue.'   On the 9th January, 1861, the Star of the West arrived off Charlestown, with men and provisions for Fort Sumpter, but the State authorities opened fire on her from the forts on Morris Island, and forced her back to sea.

"A few shots from Fort Sumpter would have settled matters; but Major Anderson scorned to imitate the *barbarity* of South Carolina, and remonstrated, whereupon Lieutenant Hall left Sumpter, accompanied by Colonel Hayne from Governor Pickens for Washington, for instructions from the President Buchanan. Hayne, instead of demanding the unconditional surrender of Fort Sumpter, simply suggested that it would be advisable to lessen the chances of collision between the Federal and State troops; but," says Mr. Ellison, " Buchanan, with a firmness in strong contrast with his (?) message, showed a determination to be neither bullied nor coaxed into treason. The ultimatum was therefore delivered to him on February 2nd, that if Fort Sumpter was not surrendered peaceably it should be taken." *

Mr. Ellison then goes on :—" Men are always more apt to follow a bad example than a good one. It is

* Ellison, p. 94.

more natural and less troublesome to fallen humanity; hence the eagerness with which the lead of South
Carolina was followed by the other Southern States."
(We could suggest another and better reason viz. self-
preservation.) " The current idea was to call a convention of all, to decide on a common course of conduct, as their grievances could be better redressed by
combined than by separate action; but the rashness
of South Carolina forced the rest to hurry out of the
Union, each independent of the rest."

Is this so? Let us see. On January 11th, Mississippi, Alabama, and Florida signed secession ordinances. Federal officers one after another sent in their
resignations to the Government. Georgia, on January 19th, passed her ordinance, by 208 votes against
89, to dissolve union between her and the other States,
under the compact entitled the Constitution of the
United States. " We, the people in convention assembled, declare and ordain that the ordinances
adopted by this State in 1788, whereby the constitution of the United States was assented to, ratified,
and adopted, and also all acts and parts of the acts
of the General Assembly ratifying and adopting
amendments to the said constitution, are hereby repealed, rescinded, and abrogated; and we further
declare that the union now subsisting between this

and other States, under the name of United States, is hereby dissolved; and that the State of Georgia is in full possession and exercise of all those rights of sovereignty which belong and appertain to a free and independent State."

January 26, Louisiana, in convention, declared herself a free and sovereign republic by ordinance of secession.

On February 1, Texas, in convention, passed a secession ordinance, by 166 against 7, which was indorsed by the popular vote, February 23.

And the natural result followed that all the world will have reason to deplore. The movement spread.

" The action of the frontier slave States had all along been on the side of moderation. Statistics prove that their citizens are more intelligent, and history shows they have been always more moderate and conservative in politics: despising the fast notions and mobocracy of the North on the one hand, and the fire-eating and filibustering doctrines of the South on the other.

" On February 4th the convention of the seceding States met at Montgomery, Alabama; and on the 7th the legislature of the State lent them $500,000. Ten delegates from Georgia, nine from Alabama, eight from South Carolina, six from

Louisiana, six from Mississippi, three from Florida signed the roll. On the 9th J. Davis was elected President, and the constitution of the Provisional Government of the Confederated States of America was issued." Mr. Ellison thus comments upon it :—
" The object is twofold. 1. To blind the world as to the real intentions of the Southern Confederacy; and 2. To give a sop to the border States, whose only inducement to retain the institution of slavery is the profit derived from the supply of Southern labour, which external slave trade would destroy. So Virginia and Co. are first coaxed, by being assured they shall have the exclusive privilege of negro breeding if they join, and threatened if they do not; the Congress may exclude importation of slaves from States not joining." The threat is empty, as there are no slaves to import from the nonjoining States, and the coaxing unnecessary, as the absolute destruction of all property in slaves, which is the watchword of the North, would of course ruin all the slaveholding proprietors in the frontier States; so it was not difficult to prognosticate which side they would take. They all joined the Confederates, and on Mr. Ellison's own showing: " They went to work quietly and business-like, and in the choice of their national leaders shunned the blustering

and blundering orators of the Palmetto State."
Why, Mr. Ellison, you told us nine pages back
they were *forced* by the rashness of the Palmetto
State.

On February 18th Davis issued his address. (See
Appendix I.)   He hoped the beginning of their
career as a separate Confederacy would not be obstructed by hostile opposition, but if such were the
case they were prepared to meet the emergency, and
maintain by the final arbitrament of the sword the
position they assumed among the nations of the
earth.

Is it their fault they were compelled to this issue,
and has not the appeal to the people been answered
to the very letter?

On February 8th, 1861, articles were drawn up
by the Confederated States.   On this dead-lock,
as it were, various compromises were offered, but
none with any effect.   The most promising was the
convention held under the presidency of the vene-
rable ex-President Tyler, on the 4th February.
The opinion of Mr. Ellison on the conduct of his
opponents is thus expressed:—

"Of the seceding States Georgia expressed her
willingness to abide by the decision of the conference, but South Carolina, with her usual amount

of fire-eating folly and contemptuous fanaticism, flatly refused to have anything to do with the proceeding. ' The separation,' she alleged, ' from the Union was final, and she had no further interest in the constitution.' " * And upon the basis of Mr. Ellison's own statement, that Lincoln and his Government never for a moment contemplated allowing her to retire, her action was not only justifiable but imperative in self-defence.

And his arguments against them are these :—

Mr. Ellison thinks " the South would not be benefited by secession. The security of the slave-owners' property would be considerably lessened. There would be no fugitive slave law acknowledged by the North. The underground railroad, now only a secret association supported by a few anti-slavery enthusiasts, in defiance of Federal law, would become a national institution, and the passengers, now numbered by units would be counted by thousands. This would breed ill-feeling between the two Confederacies, the probable result would be war, and the certain effects—defeat of the South—and a further negro stampede." Why this is the very result the South have seceded to avoid, and they may

* Ellison, p. 135.

be trusted to seeure their property themselves. " 2. The geographical extent of the two sections would be pretty nearly equal. The free States, hemmed in by Canada on the north and the slave Confederacy of the south, would have no room for expansion; and should the South Confederacy attempt to extend its empire the movement would be opposed by the North. The retention of the balance would be a constant theme of debate, if not of strife. The sickly republics of Central America would be protected by England and France, and Cuba be lost for ever to the South." A pretty argument for Englishmen to read as a reason why the South should not assert their independence!

Foremost amongst the obstacles to freedom is the money question. No emancipation can be entertained by even the least conservative slave State, which does not in some way provide compensation. Of $2,936,090,737 real and personal estate in 1850 more than half was the value of slaves at $500 per head. Since then slave property has increased 100 per cent., and the number is now four millions. So that to pay would require $3,000,000,000 or £660,000,000. It is palpable, therefore, that to confiscate all this property is impossible, and the compensation equally so. Governor

Hammond, years ago, put it to Thomas Clarkson:
"Were ever any people, civilised or savage, per-
suaded by argument, human or divine, to surrender
voluntarily $2,000,000,000? The idea is absurd.
Away then with your pretended moral suasion!
You know it is mere nonsense."

The President Lincoln's inaugural was a puzzler.
But Mr. Ellison has no difficulty in fathoming
its abstruseness, upon Punch's principle of prophe-
sying the winner of the Derby on the Thursday.
So that the anticipation of Mr. Iverson seems to
have been pretty accurately realised.*

"People read Lincoln's message and re-read it
without being able to arrive at any satisfactory conclusion: some said it meant coercion, others, concession; some peace, others war. Many who read it
to-day and pronounced it a pacific document, reversed
their opinion with a second reading on the morrow,
and *vice versâ;* but such was the helpless condition
of Government that to have laid bare the plans it
intended to carry out under certain contingencies,
would have resulted in certain disaster to the Union.
For whilst the secessionists had been long preparing
for war, Government was as unprepared as it possi-

* Vide p. 111.

bly could be.   To suppose they for a moment ever contemplated to allow the seceding States to withdraw peacefully is absurd."*   Pretty morality this! Jefferson Davis and his cabinet did not fail to apprehend the real import of their intentions, and forthwith strengthened their various military positions, and bombarded Fort Sumpter.   On the 15th of April the war proclamation was issued by Lincoln, which will be found in the Appendix (I.) with Davis's counter one.   And on the same day the Governor of Virginia announced his intention of resisting the invasion of his State, and on the 19th the Federal troops were compelled to destroy the arsenal at Harper's Ferry, and on the 20th the Gosport navy yard, Norfolk.   On the 29th the seaboard of the South was blockaded: one by one the border States came into the secession movement.   On May 6th Arkansas passed her ordinance. On June 8th Tennessee, North Carolina adding a loan of $5,000,000 to the Confederacy.   Since then military possession alone holds in the Union Missouri, Maryland, Delaware, and Western Virginia; and yet Mr. Ellison tells us, p. 292,—"The uprising does not extend to the whole people, but is entirely the work of a band of

* Ellison, p. 275.

disappointed and defeated politicians. These men have usurped the reins of Government, and now tyrannise over the peaceful and Union-loving people, and are so thoroughly organised that they can prevent the expression of opinions contrary to their notions. The real disunion party is a very small minority; there is a strong anti-secession party which is coerced and the great bulk of the people deluded, victims of foulest misrepresentations of the North's intentions, and the most absurd statements of those of European powers. If once relieved from the presence and power of traitors there will be a general reaction in favour of union; and when the people have seen the true character of the movement they will hurl rebel leaders with probably less ceremony than would be employed by the Federal Government !!!!!!" *

* The manner in which these constitutional repressors of rebellion are conducting warfare, may be seen by the atrocious piracy of one Lieut. Budd of the U.S. Navy, who lately landed and destroyed private property on the Potomac, upon no pretence whatever known to modern warfare. Here is his report :—" Dr. Hooe's house presented marks of a recent stampede" (no wonder, and thank God some escaped !) " and that some of the fugitives were females. It was richly furnished, and contained a valuable library, all of which fell a prey to the flames. Dr. Hooe was killed by a shot from a rifled cannon." Good God, is this the way warfare is to be carried on in the 19th century?

Of Mr. Ellison's fairness in weighing the relative merits of the Southern and Northern politicians we may take this as a specimen:—

"The poor whites are compelled from necessity to some labour, such as retail business, grocery stores, &c.; large numbers lounge about the country, subsisting on fishing and hunting, and odd jobs on plantations. All are held in great contempt by the slaveholding class. The Hon. G. Lumpkin, of Georgia, speaks of them as ' degraded, half-fed, half-clothed, ignorant, and without just appreciation of character.'

" And this," says Ellison, " must ever be the condition of a society where the basest features of human nature have no check, but, on the contrary, are urged into full and fiendish development, so long as the first principles of humanity are daily violated by the man-floggings and woman-beatings, the libertinism and other villanies of the slave system of the South."*

Well done Mr. Lumpkin: ominous title! With such writers arguments must be utterly thrown away; but, surely, there must be men in the North who regret such very poor abuse as this should be suffered

* Ellison, p. 187.

to inflame minds already aggravated by a sense of injustice, and who deplore in secret, apparently, for none have yet had the courage to denounce it, the virulent and bitter hatred of all the talent and statesmanship which the South has for half a century dedicated to the service of the general commonwealth. It seems impossible to believe that writers such as these can represent the feelings, or embody the sentiments of the merchants, the manufacturers, the traders, the professional men, and statesmen of such communities as Boston, Philadelphia, and New York. Or is the tyrant howl of a senseless mob drowning their voice? We fear so!

What are we to think of such a recommendation as this, which appeared but a few days ago in one of the leading journals of New York? "Instead of shedding the blood of our FELLOW-MEN! ! ! let us, North and South, unite to resent the threatened interference of England. Let one half Northern and one half Southern army join hands in a common cause, and proceed *directly* to drive the British power out of Canada. We have the strength, why not the will?"

The only parallel to this delicious suggestion is to be found in the pages of the revolutionary press of France in 1793, and based on precisely the same assumption.

I have thus taken the pains to show how completely the advocates of the Federal party ignore the facts of the Southern secession, and gloss over the character of the warfare forced on the Confederate States by the armed invasion of their land. They will not believe the South is united and firmly determined to wage war to the uttermost in defence of their homes and hearths; they ignore the refusal to treat with the commissioners sent by Davis, in the hope of averting this dreadful quarrel, and cling desperately to the notion that a large mass of non-slaveholding whites are coerced by the slaveocracy, and only thirsting for deliverance at the hands of the Northern sympathisers. Not only is this not the fact, and there is not a tittle of evidence they have attempted to show for it, but the very contrary is clear. Davis possesses the confidence of the whole of the seceding States; his requisitions are promptly attended to, his forces rapidly augmented. He has been refused all means of arbitration but the sword, and we have seen how able he is to wield it. Not less significant is the solemn and affecting thanksgiving to the God of battles just offered by the Congress of the Confederate States on their late victory. The tone and temper of the speeches of the cabinet of the North, their uniform and regular course of conduct towards the South, their seizing the moment of the secession to pass the obnoxious Morill Tariff, and the bitterness with which they inaugurated their armed invasion of their brethren, all tend to justify the stand made against them, and yet Mr. Ellison says: —

" At present there is no doubt that justice and right are on the side of the North. One great proof of the innate weakness—ay, badness—of the cause of the Southern Confederacy is the fact that it has refused to accept all constitutional remedies for its real or supposed grievances, and has preferred to hew itself out of the Union amidst the blood and carnage of civil war. There was no need for the sword to have been drawn; the ballot-box could have settled the question, if only it had been allowed fair play. If the slave-owners are honest, if their cause is founded on justice and the common weal of the Southern people, why have they refused to allow their own people to vote on the adoption or not of the new Constitution? If their grievances are what they avow them to be, why not put them in a series of constitutional amendments, and lay them before the people of the whole Union, to accept or reject as they pleased? If, under such circumstances, they failed in obtaining redress, then the world would wish them God-speed in defending their rights by means of the sword. As it is they are rebels; and even if they succeed in establishing their separate existence, the civil war which *they* have inaugurated will ever remain a foul blot upon their fame."

Now every single fact loudly gives the lie to this assumption. Who began this wretched civil war? Who were the first invaders? Was any chance left for a fair and peaceable solution given by the Federal Government? Can Mr. Ellison quote one single instance of the North granting a proposition demanded by the South? What evidence is there of coercion of public opinion by tyrannising politicians in the South? What has moved the border States to declare constitutionally against the North? What has been the action of the paternal government in those countries occupied by their troops? Where are there any signs of reaction in favour of the Union? Until these questions are fairly answered we must decline to accept such lame and clumsy declamation. It is of a piece with the mad impertinence of Mr. Cassius M. Clay, or that reverend gentleman, Mr. Maclintock, from Paris, who had the unblushing effrontery to tell us *of the tears shed in America over the mutiny of India by men who sympathised with England in her agony.* We know the ring of such metal.

CHAP. V.

THE AUTHORITIES ON THE QUESTION.

I WILL now sum up the amount of evidence we have been able to adduce. On the side of the North enough and to spare has been written, and the only fear I have is that my judgment may not have been warped by the outrageous advocacy adopted by its panegyrists. On the other side we have the message of the President of the Confederate States which will be found in *extenso* in the Appendix. But the arguments seem to be mainly these — 1. That the Federal Government is sovereign ; — which it plainly is not. 2. That the States have no right to resist its action ; — which all previous experience expressly denies. 3. That there were no circumstances to justify the secession in this case ; — on the contrary, the facts prove that if the South had not seized the present opportunity, in ten years' time they would have found themselves subjugated ; first, by the annihilation of their social status against their will and without compensation ; and, secondly,

by having their whole commerce swallowed up by re-
strictive and prohibitory protection tariffs.　4. That
the manner of secession was illegal;—but the declaration of independence put forward by the seces-
sionist was as solemn and grave a state paper as
ever issued from the bureau of any minister, and
the force and action was on the part of the North to
the complete exclusion of any pacific solution of the
differences existing in fact.　5. That the acts of the
Federal Government are in accordance with the
will of the people;—this the almost universal de-
fection of the border States expressly denies.　They
are the most statesmanlike, steady, and intelligent
subjects of the Union, and their action has, without
exception, invariably decided constitutional questions up to the present hour.　Again, the procla-
mations of martial law in Baltimore and Missouri,
the suspension of habeas corpus, and the utter extinction of any but military rule, seem to leave small
opportunity for the expression of popular will.
Lastly, there has been no one occasion for the constitutional expression of such will afforded to the
people, whereby they could legitimately affirm or
deny the legality of the action of Government which
at present has been done *mero motu*.　On all these
points, therefore, the balance lies incontestibly on

the side of the South. Commercially speaking, it does not require an elaborate argument to prove that the liberation of the splendid seaboard possessed by the Confederate States and the enormous natural resources of their country from the Northern protection, which compels them both in exports and imports to pay large profits to the Eastern seaports, who act as middlemen between foreign manufacturers and Southern producers, must be of incalculable advantage to England and France; nor are they unaware of it.

Financially the question of this miserable war is one of a few months. If the North cannot crush their foes without delay, the spirit which now pervades them will increase in intensity and force; the horror inspired by such a murder as that perpetrated on Dr. Hooe by Lieutenant Budd will rouse them into ungovernable fury, and preclude all possible settlement except by wars of extermination.

The compromise tariff of 1833 calmed the public mind at the South, but it caused a feeling of resentment in the North, that has never ceased to seek revenge, and a restoration of the high protective system. If evidence were wanting to prove that the financial question underlies the agitation at the North against the South, the passage of the

Morill Tariff immediately after the secession of the cotton States, leaving the Protectionists with a clear majority, would be sufficient. The compromise tariff of 1833 provided for a gradual reduction of customs' duties annually, untill 1840, when no more than 20 per cent, *ad valorem,* was to be collected. In 1842 the protective system was revived. The protective principle was again asserted by the *ad valorem* tariff of 30 per cent. in 1846, which was reduced to 24 per cent. in 1857. Northern shipping will no longer have the exclusive monopoly of the coasting trade of the Southern States, or be protected by high tonnage duties in Southern ports against foreign competition. Southern commerce with Europe, which has hitherto been forced through the port and city of New York, must hereafter pass directly between the Southern ports and those of Europe, augmented by the vast amount of exchangeable commodities which have hitherto been monopolised by the Northern States under the operations and effects of the protective system.

The movement of Northern and European merchandise south from New York and other northern cities having been cut off, the Confederate States must hereafter look to Europe for supplies; and if the growing crops of cotton, tobacco, and other products are to be exchanged for European goods, it is of the utmost importance that an unchecked and unrestrained intercourse should be immediately established between Southern ports and those of Europe. The summer, autumn, and winter supplies are wanted before the crops come in, and if they can be sent forward in time to meet the wants of the country, the export of specie to pay for them next winter may be avoided. It will readily be perceived that the consumption of the country must go on gradually, and that time is required to distribute supplies to a whole people inhabiting a country of such vast extent.

The South, with the full knowledge of the injurious operation of the protection system, consented to its imposition as a sacrifice. It has ever been watchful of the progress of the Union, and alternately leaned to the side of the Federation when it was too weak, and to that of the States when it was too strong. The constitution of the Federal States provided that the Federal Government, while it had the right to levy taxes upon all the property of the country for its own use, also conferred upon it the exclusive right to levy taxes upon imports. This right has been the surest bond of Union. The taxes laid under it were originally for revenue purposes only. The manufactures of the country were unimportant, and New England interests being commercial, free trade was the rule, and very low duties were imposed. It followed, as a matter of course, that that resource of revenue failed altogether in times of embargo and war, while these circumstances gave an impulse to manufactures. At the peace of 1815, the Government was $120,000,000 in debt; its revenues were small; its credit not great; and the effort to raise money by direct taxation brought it in conflict with the States in many respects. Instead of employing its own tax-gatherer, it apportioned the amount upon the States, and it was then at their mercy to pay or not; there were no means of enforcing payment. In this state of affairs the Government became very weak, and was in danger of falling to pieces. It was then that Mr. Calhoun came forward and devised a tariff, which not only gave large revenues to the Government, making it independent of the States, and enabling it to pay off its debt $10,000,000 per annum, but gave great protection to manufactures. He devised what was called the *minimum* system, by which merchandise was to pay *ad valorum* down to a certain point, below which the duty should not fall. Thus, cottons were to pay 20 per cent. duty, as long as the duty amounted to more than 6 cents per yard: but the duty was

not to be less than 6 cents. This was a great boon
to New England manufacturers, as well as a great
and indispensable aid to the Federal Government,
but a great sacrifice to the South, where the consumers of goods were to pay the duty. Nevertheless, it was a tribute to patriotism, though Mr.
Seward numbers it among the "concessions" of the
North to the South. Mr. Calhoun received un-
measured abuse for his pains from the North, where
the interests were then navigation, and Daniel
Webster was the great apostle of free trade. A
very few years served to make those two statesmen
change places. Under Mr. Calhoun's tariff the
New England manufacturers prospered rapidly;
that interest came to predominate over the commercial interest, and became clamorous for more protection. Daniel Webster, accordingly, became a
protectionist in 1824, and the tariff was raised.
Success stimulated cupidity, and the " black tariff "
of 1828 marked the growth of abuse. The power
of the Eastern manufacturers had become prodi-
gious ; the Federal debt was nearly paid off, the
finances redundant, and power was rapidly concentrated at the expense of the States. The tendency
of the Federation, which had been centrifugal in
1815, had become alarmingly centripetal in 1830.
It was then that Mr. Calhoun again stepped forth.

He stated that the South had cheerfully paid the enormous burdens of duties on imports when Northern manufacturers were young, and the Government weak; they had continued to pay them sixteen years; the manufacturers had become rich and the Government strong — so strong that State rights were being merged into its overshadowing power; he therefore demanded a recognition of State rights, and an amelioration of those burdens that the South had so long borne. To the resistance of South Carolina, under his lead, the country owes the compromise tariff of 1832, by Henry Clay.

By this compromise the duties were to undergo biennial reduction, until a common level of 20 per cent. should be reached on all goods in 1842. Before that year financial revulsion made more revenue necessary for the welfare of the Union, and the South again assented to an increase in import duties, making another of Mr. Seward's " concessions of the South."

The mode of Northern " concession " shows itself in the disposition of the territory of Louisiana, on the occasion of the admission of Missouri into the Union. That territory was all slave territory. The North demanded a division of it, so that the Northern half should become free. The South assented. New territory being afterwards acquired, the South proposed a division again, and the North refused the South any share of it. This is called a " concession " of the North. Thus Mr. Seward states :—

" In the field of Federal politics, slavery, deriving unlooked-for advantage from commercial changes, and energies unforeseen from the facilities of combination between members of the slaveholding class, and between that class and other property classes, early rallied, and has at length made a stand, not merely to retain its original defensive position, but to extend its sway throughout the whole Union. It is certain that the slaveholding class of American citizens indulge this high ambition, and that they derive encouragement for it from the rapid and effective political successes which they have already obtained. The plan of operation is this: by continued appliances of patronage, and threats of disunion, they will keep a majority favourable to these designs in the Senate, where each State has an equal representation. Through that majority they will defeat, as they best can, the admission of free States, and secure the admission of slave States. Under the protection of the Judiciary, they will, on the principle of the Dred Scott case, carry slavery into all the territories of the United States now existing and hereafter to be organised. By the action of the President and the Senate, using the treaty-making power, they will annex foreign slaveholding states. In a favourable conjuncture they will induce Congress to repeal the Act of 1808, which prohibits the foreign slave-trade, and so they will import from Africa, at the cost of only $20 a head, slaves enough to fill up the interior of the continent. Thus, relatively increasing the number of slave States, they will allow no amendment to the constitution prejudicial to their interest; and so, having permanently established their power, they expect the Federal Judiciary to nullify all State laws which shall interfere with internal or foreign commerce in slaves. When the free States shall be sufficiently demoralised to tolerate these designs, they reasonably conclude that that slavery will be accepted by those States themselves."

One has only to compare this with facts to expose its entire untruth.

When we consider that in 1816, at the commencement of the protective system, the Northern States were almost destitute of agricultural products for exportation, that their coal and iron mines were almost unknown, and that they had, comparatively, little commerce except the fisheries and the carrying trade, and from that period their manufacturing and commercial industry have increased and kept pace *precisely* with the growth of Southern agriculture, we can readily perceive the causes which have produced the great accumulation of wealth in the Northern section of the Union. It has been shown that through the instrumentality of that system the Northern States have secured to themselves great profits on all branches of their industry, and the entire monopoly of Southern commerce, both foreign and domestic.

From these causes principally an astonishing development of manufacturing industry has grown up in the Northern States since the peace of 1815 under the influence of the protective system, which, by imposing high duties on foreign goods, operated as a bounty on all domestic fabrics, and gave to Northern manufacturers control of the Southern market at an average profit of 25 per cent. on the sale of their manufactured goods.

Duties were laid on foreign tonnage coming into the ports of the United States, and foreign vessels were excluded from all participation in the coasting trade ; and, as seamen were necessary to supply the increasing tonnage of the Northern States, large bounties were offered to those engaged in the cod and mackerel fisheries, on the plea that it was necessary to establish a nursery or school of seamen for national maritime defence.

The operation of these tariffs was to tax the consumers in the South and West, *pro ratâ*, upon what manufactures they purchased of the East, and by so doing, to increase eastern capital at the expense of those other sections. The articles mostly protected, and of which the cost is enhanced to the consumers, in proportion to the duties, are manufactured at the East to the extent of $320,000,000, of which $200,000,000 are sold South and West. This gives an annual drain of $50,000,000 from the consumers of those sections, as a bonus or protection to the capital employed in manufacturing at the North. The claim for this protection is based upon the necessity of protecting home manufactures against the overwhelming capital of England. The manufactures of the South and West have to contend, however, not only against the overwhelming capital of New England, created in manufactures, but against the drain of capital from each locality, caused by the protection to Eastern goods.

The South will not, like the North, however, have provincial markets to supply, but having all within its own border, will annually diminish its purchases from the North. It will have foreign markets for its surplus. The countries of South America and Asia will be open to it, and if it there encounter British and New England competition, it will have the advantage of having, unprotected, developed its manufactures in face of the competition of Northern goods in the home market, and therefore become able to meet those goods in any market. If in a few years it does not become a seller of cotton goods to the North on a large scale, as it already is on a small scale, since Georgia, and Alabama cottons are favourites in New York, it will take none from them. The North will, however, still require food and materials, and the scale of dependence may vibrate.

The sales of Northern manufactures to the South, as parts of the offset to the large receipts of Southern produce, may be placed at $150,000,000, and from the West at possibly $30,000,000; making $180,000,000 worth of domestic merchandise purchased by the South, in addition to the imported goods.

It certainly is one of the most extraordinary spectacles of the age, to see a great, intelligent, and manufacturing people voluntarily permitting a few political aspirants to attack their best customer, and seek to destroy his means of purchase, and merely for a chimera. The French Emperor has proclaimed

that France alone " goes to war for an idea."   But
America presents the spectacle of a people who go
to destruction for an " idea."   That political party
which threatens with fire and sword every Southern
hearth, with violent death every Southern man, and
with dishonour every Southern female, amid a satur-
nalia of blood, receives countenance from merchants,
whose trade depends upon the goodwill of their
threatened neighbours, and yet vainly hope that
they will continue to buy Northern wares, and make
no effort to prepare for that hour which the tendency of that party, for the last thirty years, makes
inevitable.

A most remarkable evidence that the increase of
Northern tonnage has depended on the increase of
the cotton crop is shown in the two periods of 1830
and 1859 :—

In 1830 the tonnage of the Northern States was   .   872,578 tons.
   The cotton crop of 1830 was .   870,415 bales.
In 1859 the tonnage was   .   .   .   .   . 4,481,436 tons.
   The cotton crop of 1859 was . 4,500,000 bales.

Other intermediate periods might be given to
show that the increase of tonnage has kept pace with
the increase of the cotton crop.

The South therefore had fairly earned a right to

the fair consideration of her constitutional position on the slavery question, and when the debate took place which first brought the present parties to a direct issue on it, such was the view taken.

At New Albany, May, 1850, Mr. Webster said:—" The constitution of the United States consists in a series of mutual agreements or compromises; one thing yielded by the South, another by the North, the general mind having been brought together and the whole agreed to. Congress has protected the commerce of the North, first, by preference by way of tonnage duties,—that higher tonnage on foreign ships has never been surrendered but in consideration of a just equivalent: so that, in this respect, without grudging or complaint on the part of the South, but generously and fairly, not by way of concession, but in the true spirit of the constitution, they enjoy an exclusive right of coasting trade. They say, in Syracuse and Boston, you set up profit against conscience. But this is a flight of fanaticism. The constitution, to keep us united, to keep flowing in our hearts a fraternal feeling, must be administered in the spirit in which it was framed."

Daniel Webster, at Buffalo, New York, May, 1851, in his speech, said:—" I hope these observations will satisfy you that I know where I am, under what responsibility I speak, and before whom I appear, and I have no desire that any word I shall say this day shall be withholden from you, or your children, or your neighbours, or the whole world; for I speak before you and before my country, and, if it be not too solemn to say so, before the great Author of all things. Gentlemen, there is but one question in this country now; or if there be others, the others are but secondary, or so subordinate that they are all absorbed in the great and leading question, and that is neither more nor less than this: Can we preserve the union of these States? — not by coercion, not by military power, not by angry controversies; — but can we of this generation, you and I, your friends and my friends, can we so preserve the union of these States by such administration of the powers of the consti- tution as shall give content and satisfaction to all who live under it, and draw us together, not by military power, but by the silken cords of mutual, fraternal, patriotic affection? That is the question, and no other. Gentlemen, I believe in party distinctions. I am a party man. There are questions belonging to party in which I am concerned, and there are opinions entertained by other parties which I repudiate. But what of all that? If a house be divided against itself it will fall, and crush everybody in it. We must see that we maintain the government which is over us. We must see that we uphold the constitution, and we must do so without regard to party. The question, fellow-citizens (and I put it to you now as the real question), the question is, whether you and the rest of the people of the great State of New York, and of all the States, will so adhere to the constitution, will so enact and maintain laws to preserve that instrument, that you will not only remain in the Union yourselves, but permit your brethren to remain in it, and help to perpetuate it. That is the question. Will you carry on measures necessary to maintain the Union, or will you oppose such measures? That is the whole point in the case. You have thirty or forty members of Congress from New York; you have your proportion in the United States Senate. We have many members of Congress from New England: will they maintain the laws that are passed for the administration of the constitution, and respect the rights of the South, that the Union may be held together; and not only that we may not go out of it ourselves, which we are not inclined to do, but that by asserting and maintaining the rights of others, they may also remain in the Union? Now, gentlemen, permit me to say that I speak of no concessions. If the South wish any concessions from me they will not get it ; not a hair's breadth of it.   If they come to my house for it, they will not find it ; and the door will be shut.   I can cede nothing.   But I say that I will maintain for them, as I will maintain for you, to the utmost of my power, and in the face of all danger, their rights under the constitution, and your rights under the constitution, and I shall never be found to falter in one or the other.   Again: but I cannot express the horror I feel at the shedding of blood in a controversy between one of their States and the Government of the United States, because I see in it, in the sight of heaven, a total and entire disruption of all those ties that make us a great and a happy people."

At Syracuse in the same year, Mr. Webster said : —" What do we hear? — of persons assembling in Massachusetts and New York, who set up themselves over the constitution, above the law, and above the decisions of the higher tribunals, and who say this law shall not be carried into effect.   You have heard it here, have you not?   Has it not been so said in the country of Onandaga? (Cries of Yes, yes.)   And have they not pledged their lives, their fortunes, and their sacred honour, to defeat its execution?   Pledged their lives, their fortunes, and sacred honour, for what?   For the violation of the law, for the committal of treason to the country? for it is treason and nothing else. I am a lawyer, and I value my reputation as a lawyer more than anything else, and I tell you, if men get together and declare a law of Congress shall not be executed in any case, and assemble in numbers to prevent the execution of such law, they are traitors, and are guilty of treason, and bring upon themselves the penalties of the law. No, no. It is time to put an end to this imposition upon good citizens, good men, and good women. It is treason, treason, treason, and nothing else; and if they do not incur the penalties of treason, it is owing to the clemency of the law's administration, and to no merit of their own. Who, and what are these men? I am amazed; some of them are clergymen, and some, I am sorry to say it, lawyers; and who the rest are, God only knows. They say the law will not be executed. Let them take care, for these are pretty bold assertions. The law must be executed, not only in carrying back the slave, but against those guilty of treasonable practices in resisting its execution. Depend upon it, the law will be executed in its spirit, and to its letter. It will be executed in all the great cities; here, in Syracuse, in the midst of the next anti-slavery convention, if the occasion shall arise; then we shall see what becomes of their lives and their sacred honour. It is not unfrequently said by a class of men, to whom I have referred, that the constitution is born of hell; that it was the work of the devil; and that Washington was a miserable bloodhound, set upon the track of the African slave. How far these words differ from words that have saluted your ears within this hall, you will judge. Men who utter such sentiments are ready at any moment to destroy the charter of our liberties, of all your happiness, and of all your hope. They are either insane, or fatally bent on mischief. The question is, therefore, whether we will sustain the Government under which we live; whether we will do justice to the Southern States, that they may have no excuse for going out of the Union? If there is anybody that will not consent that the South shall have a fair hearing, a fair trial, a fair decision upon what they think the constitution secures to them, I am not of that number. Everybody knows that I am a Northern man, born in the extreme North, bred and brought up in notions altogether irreconcilable to human slavery; and why should I have any sentiments in common with the South on that subject? But when it is put to me as a public man, whether the people of the South, under the stipulations of the constitution, have not the right of a fair law from Congress for returning to them the fugitive? I say they have, and I could not say otherwise."

At Albany, New York:—"I yet believe firmly, that this Union, once broken, is utterly incapable, according to all human experience, of being reconstructed in its original character, of being re-cemented by any chemistry, or art, or effort, or skill of man."

May 21*st*, 1850.—Mr. Clay said:—"A dissolution of the Union, the greatest of all calamities, in my opinion, which can befal this country, may not in form take place; but next to that is a dissolution of those fraternal and kindred ties that bind us together as one free, Christian, and commercial people. In my opinion the body politic cannot be preserved unless this agitation, this distraction, this exasperation which is going on between the two sections of the country, shall cease; unless it do cease, I am afraid that this Union, for all the high and noble purposes for which our fathers formed it, will not be preserved. Mr. Douglas said the real object and true intent was to re-organise in the territories the great principle of self-government, in obedience to which the people of each State and territory coming into the Union should decide for themselves what kind of institutions and laws were best adapted to their condition and welfare. It was in obedience to this great principle, in defence of which the battles of the revolution were fought,—the principle for the preservation of which the constitution of the United States was adopted,— the principle of popular rights and State equality which underlies our whole system of representative government, — for the preservation of this great principle it was that the Washington and Nebraska bills were passed in the form in which they now appear on the statute book."

Feb. 19*th*, 1850. — Senator Downs: — " By the event of a dissolution of the Union, still we would be better off than the North, and could better provide for ourselves. We would have that with which man originally started in this world, — a virgin soil and plenty of hands to work it, — the South having a rich country and a delightful climate. Sir, this is a subject not for me, nor for those from whom I came, to discuss or to look to ; but it is one fraught with results so important, that I do hope that our brethren in the North, who are so deeply interested in it, will turn their attention to it, will cast up the accounts, and will see exactly where and how they stand before they proceed further in their *labour of dissolving the Union.*"

March 11*th*, 1850.—William H. Seward :—" We

denounce the principles of the law for the recapture
of fugitives, therefore, unjust, unconstitutional, and
immoral; and thus, while patriotism withholds its
approbation, the conscience of our people condemns
it. You will say that these convictions of ours are
disloyal. Grant it for the sake of argument. They
are, nevertheless, honest: and the law is to be executed among us, not among you; not by us, but by
the Federal authority. Has any Government ever
succeeded in changing the moral convictions of its
subjects by force? But these convictions imply no
disloyalty. We reverence the constitution, although
we perceive this defect, just as we acknowledge the
splendour and the power of the sun, although its
surface is tarnished with here and there an opaque
spot. Your constitution and laws convert hospitality to the refugee from the most degrading
oppression on earth, into a crime; but all mankind
except you esteem that hospitality a virtue. The
right of extradition of a fugitive from justice, is not
admitted by the law of nature and of nations, but
rests in voluntary compacts. And here is the other:
' No person held to service or labour in one State,
and under the laws thereof, escaping into another,
shall, in consequence of any laws or regulation
therein, be discharged from such service or labour,

but shall be delivered up on claim of the party to whom such service or labour is due.'

" This is from the constitution of the United States in 1787, and the parties were the Republican States of this Union. The law of nations disavows such compacts; the law of nature, written in the hearts and consciences of freemen, repudiates them. Armed power could not enforce them, because there is no public conscience to sustain them.

" I must tell you, nevertheless, in candour and in plainness, that the spirit of the people of the free States is set upon a spring, that it rises with the pressure put on it. That spring, if pressed too hard, will give a recoil that will not leave here one servant who knew his master's will and did it not. You will say this implies violence. Not at all; it implies only peaceful, lawful, constitutional customary action. I cannot too strongly express my surprise that those who insist that the people of the slave States cannot be held back by remedies outside of the constitution, should so far misunderstand us of the free States, as to suppose we would not exercise our constitutional rights to sustain the policy which we deem just and beneficent. The constitution regulates our stewardship; the constitution devotes the domain to union, to justice, to defence, welfare, and to liberty. But there is a higher law than the constitution, which regulates our authority over the domain, and devotes it to the same noble purposes.

" Let, then, those who distrust the Union make compromises to save it. I shall not impeach their wisdom, as I certainly cannot their patriotism, but indulging no such apprehensions myself, I shall vote for the admission of California directly without conditions, without qualifications, and without compromises. The Union,—the creature of necessities, physical, moral, social, and political, — endures by virtue of the same necessities; and these necessities are stronger than when it was produced; stronger by the greater amplitude of territory now covered by it; stronger by sixfold increase of the society living under its beneficent protection; stronger by the augmentation, ten thousand times, of the fields, the workshops, the mines, and the ships of that society,—of its productions of the sea, of the plough, of the loom, and the anvil, in their constant circle of internal and international exchange; stronger in the long rivers penetrating regions before unknown; stronger in all the artificial roads, canals, and other channels and avenues essential not only to trade but to defence; stronger in steam navigation, in steam locomotion on the land, and in the telegraphic communications unknown when the constitution was adopted; stronger in the freedom and in the growing empire of the seas; stronger in the element of national honour in all lands: and stronger than all in the now settled habits of veneration and affection for institutions so stupendous and so useful."

March 11*th*, 1850.—Mr. Webster:—" It is not to be denied that we live in the midst of strong agitations, and are surrounded by very considerable dangers to our institutions of government.   The imprisoned minds are let loose; the East, the West, the North, and the stormy South all combine to throw the whole ocean into commotion, to toss its billows to the skies, and to disclose its profoundest depths.   I do not affect to regard myself, Mr. President, as holding, or as fit to hold the helm in this combat of the political elements; but I have a duty to perform, and I mean to perform it with fidelity, not without a sense of surrounding dangers, but not without hope.   I have a part to act, not for my own security or safety, — for I am looking out for no fragment upon which to float away from the wreck, if wreck there must, — but for the good of the whole and the preservation of the whole; and there is that which will keep me to my duty during this struggle, whether the sun and the stars shall appear or shall not appear for many days. I speak to-day for the preservation of the Union; 'hear me for my cause.' I speak to-day, out of a solicitous and anxious heart, for the restoration to the country of that quiet and that harmony which make the blessings of this Union so rich and so dear to us all.

" I will not state what might produce the disruption of these States; but, Sir, I see it as plainly as I see the sun in heaven, I see that disruption must produce such a war as I will not describe in its twofold characters,—peaceable reaction, peaceable reaction ! — the concurrent agreement of all the members of this great Republic to separate."

March 2nd. — Mr. Chase * : — " I cannot believe there is danger in such a course. Least of all does the stale cry of disunion alarm me. Men generally adapt remedies to evils; but what evil that the slave States complain of will disunion cure? Will it establish slavery in the territories? Will it procure the return of fugitives? Will it suppress discussion ? Will it secure slavery where it is? Sir, all men must see that disunion is no remedy for the slave States. Why the cry, if not to alarm the timid, the sensitive, the unreflecting — to afford excuses for concession—

* Now Secretary of State to President Lincoln.

and thus secure advantages which the sober judgment and enlightened consciences of the country
would never yield? Mr. President, I have never
calculated the value of the Union. Nor are these
the sentiments of Ohio alone. They are the sentiments of the people throughout the free States.
Here and there the arts or the fears of politicians or
capitalists may suppress their utterance, but they
live, and will live, in the hearts of the many. It
may be, however, that you will succeed here in
sacrificing the claims of freedom by some settlement
carried through the forms of legislation; but the
people will unsettle your settlement. It may be
that you will determine that the territories shall
not be secured by law against the ingress of slavery;
the people will reverse your determination. It
may be that you will succeed in burying the ordinance of freedom; but the people will write upon
its tomb, 'Resurgam:' and the same history which
records its resurrection may also inform posterity
that they who fancied they had killed the proviso,
only committed political suicide."

Such was the view taken by the most able as
well as the most temperate of the statesmen who
then swayed public opinion. They considered the
Government was trustee for the whole nation, and
that law and constitutional right should govern the

decision of the legislature, and not the peculiar feeling or conscience of any party or section. Curiously enough, the argument that the States had a right to exercise such a resistance and controverting power to the general Government, as is now asserted and acted on in self-defence by the South, was brought forward then by the very men who now so loudly denounce it.

Here are their solemn appeals to Congress:—

Mr. Wade:—" If this great people cannot find it to be their common interest to keep together, I know full well they will not remain united. The very moment a majority of the North and South shall find that it is incompatible with their interest to be united, they will separate, and nothing can prevent it. Let me assure gentlemen that nothing will lead to such a result sooner than the introduction of bills of this description, without any regard to the feelings and principles of the free North."

Mr. W. H. Seward said:—" I warn you, senators, that you are saving this Union at a fearful cost. This is a republican government, the first and only one that has ever been widely and permanently successful. Every man in this country, every man in Christendom, who knows anything of the philosophy of government, knows that this Republic has been thus successful only by reason of the stability, strength, and greatness of the individual States. You are saving the union of those States by tapping and undermining the columns on which it rests. You reply to all this, that there is a newly-developed necessity for this act of Federal aggrandisement."

Mr. Sumner said:—" Suffice it to say that it is an intrusive and offensive encroachment on State rights, calculated to intervent the power of the States in the protection of the liberties of their citizens. This Act is made the occasion of a new assault on State rights. It is an assumption, by Congress, of power not delegated to it under the constitution, and an infraction of rights secured to the States. For myself, let me say that I look with no pleasure on any possibility of conflict between the State and national jurisdictions, but I trust that if the interests of freedom so require, the States will not hesitate."

August 12*th.*—Mr. Berrion, of Georgia, in the U.S. Senate, said:—" But this much I have to say, that whether secession be a right, resulting from the nature of our federal compact, or must be considered as revolutionary in its nature—the *ultima ratio* of an oppressed people; whether it result from the provisions of the constitution, or belong to the principle of self-government; whether it be one or the other, whether it be a right to be exercised under the constitution, or an act amounting to revolution—

whichever it be, whenever two, three, four, or half
a dozen States of the Union shall resolve upon per-
forming that act, call it what you will, whether revolution, or constitutional and peaceful retirement
from the Union, whenever that act shall be performed
the Union will be at an end. I do not know if the
enunciation of this opinion may constitute treason;
I do not know if it indicates that I am a disunionist;
if the first, I have to say that the treason to which
it may amount is of modern date, and should be
comprised among the irregularities which attend the
admission of California; if the latter, if it be supposed to be the opinion of a disunionist, I have only
to appeal to the history of my past life, humble and
unambitious as it has been, and as it will be, to repel
so unfounded an imputation. It is because of my
attachment and devotion to the Union that I express
the opinion. It is because of my fear that the measure which you are passing may drive some of these
States to an act which will, in my judgment, inevitably result in disunion; it is because of these apprehensions that I venture to express to you this
opinion and these fears. I ask you, then, to pause.
I have said to you before that I do not believe this
Union can be preserved by the use of bayonets; I do
not believe the menace of military force in any

possible contingency is calculated to allay the excited feelings of the American people.   No, Sir; the disunionist is that man who uses the means by which the existing excitement, even though it were misguided, may be increased to an extent which will place the question of the Union beyond our control. Your army and your navy have been referred to to alarm us.   Sir, they can enforce your laws upon individuals; but your military force, great as it is, can never coerce sovereign States to remain in this Union, when they have resolved no longer to do so. I know their gallantry and their patriotism; and especially I know, and am willing to render a cheerful tribute to, the skill, and gallantry, and patriotism, and the public and private virtues of the distinguished man at the head of that army, with whom the South has been menaced. Sir, that distinguished chieftain has been victorious on many a field; his military life has been a series of triumphs; but there is one battle-field—God forbid that he should ever be called to it—on which he has never won, on which he can never win, a trophy.   That is the field on which, commanding American soldiers, he shall encounter American citizens battling in defence of their insulted home and violated rights."

Mr. Pratt, Maryland:—" I read this morning the abstract of a speech delivered by a member of this body (Mr. Seward) before the people of a non-slaveholding State of this Union, which shows the character of the aggressions which have excited the feelings of the South upon this subject. Permit me to read two extracts from that speech, and ask the attention of those senators who, at one time, were disposed to protect the individual referred to from the just censure which his remarks, made in this body, ought to have imposed upon him, by the sentiments expressed by him on this occasion:—' It is written ' (says he) ' in the constitution of the United States that five slaves shall count as equal to three freemen as a basis of representation ; and it is written also in violation of the Divine law, that we shall surrender the fugitive slave, who takes a refuge at our firesides from his relentless pursuers.' Then his advice is, ' Reform your own code.' This is the advice given to the people of Ohio, a non-slaveholding State, at a mass meeting, and given to a people who have produced as much of this excitement on the subject of fugitive slaves as those of any other State. This is the advice given to the people by one standing high in the estimation of his own State. ' Reform your own code, extend a cordial welcome to the fugitive who lays his weary limbs at your door, and defend him as you would your household gods.'   Yes, Sir, 'defend him as you would your household gods."

Mr. Foot.—" What senator do you allude to ?"

Mr. Cass.—" The higher law."

Mr. Pratt.—" That is it.   Now, I ask those senators who represent the non-slaveholding States of this Union, can you expect that the great object which the Senate has had in view for the last six months, that of producing peace and harmony between the people of the two sections of this Union, can be attained ? "

Inasmuch as political power was the evident cause of the movements of either party in the struggles that took place both in the legislature, and also in the States where the outrages took place, on the same plea as was urged for the policy in its leaders' speeches, it behoves us to test the conduct of both, by the tone adopted by the acknowledged leaders of each, as well as the facts of the alleged violence in the States where the conflict arose, as far as the evident bias of the reports allows us to extricate the truth.   I will not adduce the opinions of any known advocate of the South; any owner of slaves, who might be open to the charge of prejudice, if not of being compelled, by his position, to colour the argument in favour of the case of the slave-owning proprietors, but I will quote from the speeches of Northern statesmen, who take up the cause of the South on what are called and are understood as "Constitutional Principles."

March 14th, 1850.—Mr. Calhoun in the Senate said:—" You have thus forced upon you the greatest and gravest question that can ever come under your consideration. If the agitation goes on, the same force, acting with increased intensity, as has been shown, will finally snap every cord, when nothing will be left to hold the States together, except force. But surely that can by no propriety of language be called a union, when the only means by which the weaker is connected with the stronger is force. Surely the connection will partake much more of the character of subjugation of the weak to the strong, than the union of free, independent, and sovereign States in one confederation as they stood in the early stages of government, and which alone is worthy the sacred name of union. There is but one way the Union can be saved, and that is by adopting such means as will satisfy the Southern States that they can remain in the Union consistently with their honour and safety, and that by removing the causes; that once done, discontent will cease, harmony and kind feeling will be restored, and every apprehension of danger to the Union removed. The Union cannot be saved by eulogies, however splendid or numerous. The cry of 'Union, Union, the glorious Union!' can no more prevent disunion, than the cry of 'Health, glorious health!' can save a patient lying dangerously ill. So long as the Union, instead of being regarded as a protector, is regarded in the opposite character, by not much less than a majority of the States, it will be in vain to attempt to conciliate them by pronouncing eulogies on it. Besides, this cry of union comes commonly from those men whom we cannot believe to be sincere—it usually comes from our assailants; and if they loved the Union they would necessarily be devoted to the constitution; it made the Union, and to destroy the constitution would be to destroy the Union. But the only reliable and certain evidence of devotion to the constitution is to abstain on the one hand from violating it, and to repel on the other all attempts to violate it. Have our assailants abstained from violating the constitution? Let the many acts passed by the Northern States to set aside and annul the clause providing for the delivering up of fugitive slaves answer. I cite this not that it is the only instance (for there are many others), but because the violation in this particular is too notorious and palpable to be denied. Again, have they stood forth faithfully to repel violation of the constitution? Let their course in reference to the agitation of the slave question, carried on for fifteen years, avowedly for the purpose of abolishing slavery, answer. I return to the question: How is the Union to be saved? Only by a full and final settlement, on the principles of justice, of all the questions at issue between the sections. The South asks for justice simply, and less she ought not to take." And on March 3rd, 1850, Mr. Calhoun said:—"I will say, and say it boldly, for I am not afraid to say the truth on such a question, that as things now stand, the Southern States cannot with safety remain in the Union. When this question may be settled, when we shall come to a constitutional understanding, is a question of time; but as matters now stand, I appeal to the Senator from Mississippi if he thinks that the South can remain in the Union upon terms of equality."

The deliberate right of the South to enjoy the property they contend is guaranteed by the law of the land, and a justification of resistance against a coercion not warranted by law, and certainly, by the plainest rule of human action, calculated to defeat any peaceable solution of the question. On the other hand, I have quoted the avowed opinions of the leaders of the present Federal Government, whose subsequent conduct has carried fully into action the sentiments they expressed.

Now, making all due allowance for the strong feelings which in the one case would naturally prompt men to exert themselves to defend what they believe to be a legal possession, and on the other compel a fearless and persistent assertion of principles and conduct which conscience impels them to consider as imperative; it will be sufficient to compare the language and tendency of the speeches to see on which side the balance of constitutional law and of sound and temperate policy plainly lies. And this becomes of more importance when we come to look at the acts which followed these discussions in the deliberative chambers. We have already alluded to the Kansas affair,—here is an accusation by an authority that cannot be safely impugned.

1856. Message of the President of the United States, Washington Franklin Pierce, of New Hampshire, December 2nd: — " To accomplish their objects they dedicate themselves to the odious task of depreciating the Government organisation, which stands in their way, and of calumniating, with indiscriminate invective, not only the citizens of particular States, with whose laws they find fault, but all others of their fellow-citizens throughout the

country who do not participate with them in their
assaults upon the constitution, framed and adopted
by our fathers, and the blessings it has conferred,
the steady support and grateful reverence of their
children. They seek an object which they well
know to be a revolutionary one. They are perfectly
aware that the change in the relative condition of
the white and black races in the slaveholding States,
which they would promote, is beyond their lawful
authority; that to them it is a foreign object; that
it cannot be effected by any peaceful instrumentality of theirs; that for them, and the States of
which they are citizens, the only path to its accomplishment is through burning cities and ravaged
fields, and slaughtered populations, and all there is
most terrible in foreign, complicated with civil and
servile war; and that the first step in the attempt is
the forcible disruption of a country, embracing in
its broad bosom a degree of liberty, and an amount
of individual and public prosperity, to which there
is no parallel in history, and substituting in its place
hostile governments, driven at once and inevitably
into mutual devastation and fratricidal carnage,
transforming the now peaceful and felicitous brother-
hood into a vast permanent camp of armed men, like
the rival monarchies of Europe and Asia. Well
knowing that such, and such only, are the means

and the consequences of their plans and purposes, they endeavour to prepare the people of the United States for civil war by doing everything in their power to deprive the constitution and the laws of moral authority, and to undermine the fabric of the Union by appeals to passions and sectional prejudice, by indoctrinating its people with reciprocal hatred, and educating them to stand face to face as enemies, rather than shoulder to shoulder as friends. It is by the agency of such unwarrantable interference, foreign and domestic, that the minds of many, otherwise good citizens, have been so inflamed into the passionate condemnation of the domestic institutions of the Southern States, as at length to pass insensibly to almost equally passionate hostility towards their fellow-citizens of those States, and thus, finally, to fall into temporary fellowship with the avowed and active enemies of the constitution. But they have entered a path which leads nowhere unless it be to civil war and disunion, and which has no other possible outlet; they have proceeded thus far in that direction, in consequence of the successive stages of their progress having consisted of a series of secondary issues, each of which professed to be confined within constitutional and peaceful limits, but which attempted indirectly what few men were willing to do directly; that is, to act aggressively against the constitutional rights of nearly one half of the thirty-one States. In the long series of acts of indirect aggression, the first was the strenuous agitation, by citizens of the Northern States, in Congress and out of it, of the question of negro emancipation in the Southern States. The second step in this path of evil consisted of acts of the people of the Northern States, and in several instances of their governments, aimed to facilitate the escape of persons held to service in the Southern States, and to prevent their extradition when reclaimed according to law, and in virtue of express provisions of the constitution. To promote this object, legislative enactments and other means were adopted to take away or defeat rights which the constitution solemnly guaranteed. In order to nullify the then existing act of Congress, concerning the extradition of fugitives from service, laws were enacted in many States forbidding their officers, under the severest penalties, to participate in the execution of any act of Congress whatever. In this way that system of harmonious co-operation between the authorities of the United States, and of the several States, for the maintenance of their common institutions, which existed in the early years of the Republic, was destroyed; conflicts of jurisdiction came to be frequent; and Congress found itself compelled, for the support of the constitution and the vindication of its power, to authorise the appointment of new officers charged with the execution of its acts, as if they and the officers of the States were the ministers, respectively, of foreign governments in a state of mutual hostility, rather than fellow-magistrates of a common country, peacefully subsisting under the protection of one well-constituted union. Thus here, also, aggression was followed by reaction; and the attacks upon the constitution at this point did but serve to raise up new barriers for its defence and security. The third stage of this unhappy sectional controversy was in connection with the organisation of territorial governments, and the admission of new States into the Union. In the progress of constitutional inquiry and reflection, it had now at length come to be seen clearly that Congress does not possess constitutional power to impose restrictions of this character upon any present or future State of the Union. In a long series of decisions on the fullest argument, and after the most deliberate consideration, the Supreme Court of the United States had finally determined this point in every form under which the question could arise, whether as affecting public or private rights, in questions of the public domain, of religion, of navigation, and of servitude. The several States of the Union are, by force of the constitution, co-equal in domestic legislative power. Congress cannot change a law of domestic relation in the State of Maine; any more can it in the State of Missouri. Any statute which proposes to do this is a mere nullity: it takes away no right, it confers none. Still, where the nominal restitution of this nature, already a dead letter in law, was in terms repealed by the last Congress, in a clause of the Act organising the territories of Kansas and Nebraska, that repeal was made the occasion of a wide-spread and dangerous agitation. It was alleged that, the original enactment being a compact of perpetual moral obligation, its repeal constituted an odious breach of faith. An Act of Congress, while it remains unrepealed, more especially if it be constitutionally valid in the judgment of those public functionaries, whose duty it is to pronounce on that point, is undoubtedly binding on the conscience of each good citizen of the Republic. But in what sense can it be asserted that the enactment in question was invested with perpetuity and entitled to the respect of a solemn compact? Between whom was the compact? No distinct contending powers of the Government, no separate sections of the Union, treating as such, entered into treaty stipulations on the subject. It was a mere clause of an Act of Congress, and, like any other controverted matter of legislation, received its final shape, and was passed by compromises of conflicting opinions or sentiments of the members of Congress. But if it had moral authority over men's consciences, to whom did this authority attach? Not to those of the North, who had repeatedly refused to confirm it by extension, and who had zealously striven to establish other and incompatible regulations upon the subject. And if, as it thus appears, the supposed compact had no obligatory force as to the North, of course it could not have any as to the South, for all such compacts must be mutual and reciprocal obligation. The position assumed, that Congress had no moral right to enact such repeal, was strange enough, and singularly so in view of the fact, that the argument came from those who openly refused obedience to existing laws of the land, having the same popular designation and quality as compromise acts; nay more, who unequivocally disregarded and condemned the most positive and obligatory injunctions of the constitution itself, and sought, by every means within their reach, to deprive a portion of their

fellow-citizens of the equal enjoyment of those
rights and privileges guaranteed alike to all by the
fundamental compact of our Union. Then followed
the cry of alarm from the North against imputed
Southern encroachments; which cry sprang in reality
from the spirit of revolutionary attack on the domestic institutions of the South. Of this last agitation
one lamentable feature was, that it was carried on
at the immediate expense of the peace and happiness
of the people of the territory of Kansas. That was
made the battle-field, not so much of opposing fac-
tions or interests within itself, as of the conflicting
passions of the whole people of the United States.
Revolutionary disorder in Kansas had its origin in
projects of intervention, deliberately arranged by
certain members of that Congress which enacted the
law for the organisation of the territory. And when
propagandist colonisation of Kansas had thus been
undertaken in one section of the Union, for the
systematic promotion of its peculiar views of policy,
then ensued, as a matter of course, a counteraction
with opposite views in other sections of the Union.
The attempt of a part of the inhabitants of the
territory to erect a revolutionary government, though
sedulously encouraged and supplied with pecuniary aid
from active agents of disorder in some of the States,

has completely failed.   Bodies of armed men, foreign to the territory, have been prevented from entering or compelled to leave it.   Predatory bands, engaged in acts of rapine, under cover of the existing political disturbances, have been worsted or dispersed.   The withdrawal of that force from its proper duty of defending the country against foreign foes, or the ravages of pirates, to employ it for the suppression of domestic insurrection, is, when the exigency occurs, a matter of the most earnest solicitude."

On March 30th, 1855, the settlers chose their legislature : 6,218 votes polled, of which 4,908 were illegal.   Two cabals were formed, one the Bogus, the other Topeke legislature ; but an end was put to the rivals by force in 1856.

A new convention, held in November, 1857, formed the Lecompton Constitution as a compromise; and in April, 1858, Congress admitted the State into the Union, with liberty to accept or reject the Lecompton Constitution.   It was rejected, and the Leavenworth Constitution passed both.

Again, the attempt of Brown and his associates on Harper's Ferry, and the means he took to accomplish it, as well as the public announcement of his views and intentions, are well worthy the attention of those who, unbiassed by any of the partisan passions which obscure the view and warp the judgment, desire fairly to consider on which side of the two parties, which now stand arrayed in internecine war, the plain measure of truth and justice is to be found. We subjoin the opinions of the leading debaters on the questions as they arose.

In the Senate, Mr. Charles Sumner said:—" And where the cry, ' I am an American citizen,' has been interposed in vain against outrage of every kind, even upon life itself. Are you against sacrilege? I present it for your execration. Are you against robbery? I hold it up to your scorn. Are you for the protection of American citizens? I show you how their dearest rights have been cloven down, while a tyrannical usurpation has sought to instal itself on their very necks! But the wickedness which I now begin to expose is immeasurably aggravated by the motives which prompt it. Not in any common lust for power did this uncommon tragedy have its origin. It is the rape of a virgin territory, compelling it to the hateful embrace of slavery; and it may be clearly traced to a depraved longing for a new slave State, the hideous offspring of such a crime, in the hope of adding to the power of slavery in the national Government. Yes, Sir, when the whole world, alike Christian and Turk, is rising up to condemn this wrong, and to make it a hissing to the nations, here in our Republic, force—ay, Sir, force— has been openly employed in compelling Kansas to this pollution, and all for the sake of political power. There is the simple fact, which you will vainly attempt to deny, but which in itself presents an essential wickedness that makes other public crimes seem like public virtues.   But this enormity, vast beyond comparison, swells to dimensions of wickedness which the imagination toils in vain to grasp, when it is understood that for this purpose are hazarded the horrors of intestine feud, not only in this distant territory, but everywhere throughout the country. Already the muster has begun; the strife is no longer local, but national.   Even now, while I speak, portents hang on all the arches of the horizon, threatening to darken the broad land, which already yawns with mutterings of civil war.   The fury of the propagandists of slavery, and the calm determination of their opponents, are now diffused from the distant territory over wide-spread communities, and the whole country, in all its extent, marshalling hostile divisions, and foreshadowing a strife, which, unless happily averted by the triumph of freedom, will become war—fratricidal, parricidal war—with an accumulated wickedness beyond the wickedness of

any war in human annals; justly provoking the
avenging judgment of Providence and the avenging
pen of history, and constituting a strife, in the language of the ancient writer, more than foreign, more
than social, more than civil; but something com-
pounded of all these strifes, and in itself more than
war. Such is the crime which you are to judge. But
the criminal also must be dragged into day, that you
may see and measure the power by which all this
wrong is sustained. From no common source could
it proceed. In its perpetration was needed a spirit
of vaulting ambition which would hesitate at nothing;
a hardihood of purpose which was insensible to the
judgment of mankind; a madness for slavery which
should disregard the constitution, the laws, and all
the great examples of our history. Justice to Kansas
can be secured only by the prostration of this influence : for this is the power behind—greater than any
President—which succours and sustains the crime.
Nay, the proceedings now amain derive their fearful consequence only from this connection. As the
senator from South Carolina is the Don Quixote,
the senator from Illinois (Mr. Douglas) is the squire
of slavery, its very Sancho Panza, ready to do all its
humiliating offices. This senator, in his laboured
address, vindicating his laboured report, piling one

mass of elaborate error upon another mass, con-
strained himself, as you will remember, to unfamiliar
decencies of speech. Of that address I have nothing
to say at this moment, though before I sit down I
shall show something of its fallacies. But I go
back now to an earlier occasion, when, true to his
native impulses, he threw into this discussion, 'for
a charm of powerful trouble,' personalities most
discreditable to this body. I will not stop to repel
the imputations which he cast upon myself; but I
mention them to remind you of the 'sweltering venom
sleeping got,' which, with other poisoned ingredients,
he cast into the cauldron of this debate. Of other
things I speak. Standing on this floor the senator
issued his rescript, requiring submission to the
usurped power of Kansas, and this was accompanied
by a manner—all his own—such as befits the
tyrannical threat. Very well; let the senator try.
I tell him now that he cannot enforce any such
submission. The senator, with the slave power at
his back, is strong; but he is not strong enough for
this purpose. He is bold, he shrinks from nothing;
but even his audacity cannot compass this work.
The senator copies the British officer, who with
boastful swagger said that, with the hilt of his sword,
he would cram the 'stamps' down the throats of the

American people; and he will meet a similar failure. He may convulse this country with civil pride. Like the ancient madman, he may set fire to this temple of constitutional liberty, grander than Ephesia's dame, but he cannot enforce obedience to that tyrannical usurpation." Mr. Cass:—" I have listened with equal regret and surprise to the speech of the honourable senator from Massachusetts. Such a speech! the most un-American and unpatriotic that ever grated on the ears of the members of this high body, as I hope never to hear again here or elsewhere. But, Sir, I did not rise to make any comments on the speech of the honourable senator, open, as it is, to the highest censure and disapprobation." *

Mr. Douglas, in reply to Mr. Sumner:—"Is there anything in the means by which he got here to give him a superiority over other gentlemen who came by the ordinary means? Is there anything to justify it in the fact that he came here with a deliberate avowal that he would never obey one clause of the constitution of the United States, and yet put his hand upon the Holy Bible, in the presence of this body, and appealed to Almighty God to witness that

* Appendix to Congressional Globe, 1855–56, May 19, p. 530.

he would be faithful to the constitution, with a pledge of perjury on his soul, by violating both that oath and the constitution? He came here with a pledge to perjure himself as the condition of eligibility to the place. Has he a right to arraign us because we have felt it to be our duty to be faithful to that constitution which he disavows — to that oath which he assumes and then repudiates? The Senate have not forgotten the debate on the fugitive slave law, when that senator said, in reply to a question whether he was in favour of carrying into effect that clause of the constitution for the rendition of fugitive slaves, ' Is thy servant a dog, that he should do this thing? A dog, to be true to the constitution of your country? A dog, to be true to your oath? A dog, unless you are a traitor !' That was his position; and still he comes here and arraigns us for crime, and talks about ' audacity !' Did mortal man ever witness such audacity in an avowed criminal? He comes here with a pledge to defy the constitution of his country, and the wrath of God, by not obeying his oath, and then talks about audacity ! In what does my audacity, of which he speaks, consist? It consists in the fact that, coming from a free State, born in a free State, with associations all around me tinctured strongly with anti-slavery,

when I was elected to the Senate, and took an oath
to be true to the constitution, I would not violate
that oath, even in obedience to a popular prejudice
at home. My crime consists in saying to my people,
' So long as that constitution requires the fugitive
slave to go back, so long will I, as a citizen, or a
representative, be faithful to that clause of the constitution as well as to every other.' I tell the people
with whom I live that I do not desire a man to represent me who, for the sake of getting an office, will
take an oath to be true to the constitution, with a
secret pledge to violate it. I do not wish to have a
man on the bench to administer justice who, in order
to get the place, will take an oath to be faithful to
the constitution, and then repudiate both the constitution and the oath. I tell my people, ' If you want
perjurers to represent you, get the men who believe
in a higher law than the constitution. I have stood
by my principles, by my pledges, by the constitution, and by my oath; if I had abandoned them, I
could have had the applause of all these black republican leaders.'

"I do not intend to-day to go into the discussion of
the Kansas question, or of the regularity of the proceeding there. I have shown on a former occasion
conclusively, that the conduct of the leaders of the

State, moreover, is an act of rebellion against the constitution and laws of the country. What is the defence? The defence is, that they are carrying out the principles of the Declaration of Independence; that they are doing what our fathers did in the revolution; that they have a right to do what our fathers did; and, hence, inasmuch as our fathers were rebels against England, they have a right to be rebels against the United States of America. That they are aiming at revolution is no longer to be disguised; 'revolution' is becoming their watch-word. And why? Because disunion is the object. Ambitious leaders are not willing to trust their political fortunes to a vote, where the North and the South vote alike for or against the same man. They must drive this point to disunion, for they now do not hope in this coming election, which has been so proudly alluded to by the senator from Massachusetts, to ruin a man who can avow his principles in one half of the States of this Union. But why not be as daring and defiant now as you were eighteen months ago, when you organised mobs to put down the freedom of speech—when you armed your bullies and sent them into democratic meetings to prevent a Nebraska man from being heard? I do not ask you to resort to the violence you then used; I prefer that you should

withdraw your secret orders for assassination, by
which the public officers of the country are being
murdered in Kansas.   I do not ask you to practise
your violence, but avow the same creed which you did
then ; that creed was the repeal of the Kansas-
Nebraska Act; the repeal of the fugitive slave law ;
the abolition of slavery in the district of Columbia ;
the abolition of the slave trade between the States;
the admission of no more territory into the Union,
unless slavery should be first prohibited." *

Mr. Wilson of Massachusetts said :—" The senator
from Texas sneers, and others may sneer, at ' bleeding Kansas,' but I tell him one thing, that the next
day at ten o'clock, after the Presidential election,
there was an assemblage of men, continuing through
two days in the city of Boston, from several States,
and from ' bleeding Kansas,'— men, some of whom
you guarded through the summer months for treason, assembled together to take measures to save
Kansas ; and I assure that senator and others who
may think this struggle for Kansas is ended with
the election, that more money has been contributed
since that election than during any three months of
the whole controversy ; thousands of garments have

* Appendix to Congressional Globe 1855-56, May 19, p. 545.

been sent to protect that suffering people. We have resolved, and we mean to keep that resolution, that if by any lawful effort, any personal sacrifice, Kansas can be saved to freedom, it shall be saved, in spite of your present administration, or anything that your incoming administration can do." *

Mr. Crawford: —" I approve every word in the message touching the subject of our constitutional rights, as well as the opinions set forth in reference to the ultimate objects to be accomplished by the gentlemen who compose the republican party, and shall endeavour to show to this House and the country that the charges are not without foundation. The President asserts that the object which you seek to accomplish you well know to be a revolutionary one; this being denied, I propose to show its truth, and in language not to be misunderstood, that interference with slavery in the States and in the territories is the primary object of ' Republican ' desire; which, accomplished by that party, would be but revolution. What perfidy and wrong has been done? Nothing more than the people of Kansas and Nebraska, just as those of Utah and New Mexico, and the people of all the territories,

* Appendix to the Congressional Globe 1856–57, in the Senate, Dec. 19, p. 65.

shall be perfectly free to form and regulate their domestic institutions in their own way, subject only to the provisions of the constitution. The tribune propose that the nation's capitol should blaze by the torch of the incendiary, rather than that the free white men of those territories should frame their institutions, subject to the constitution; his regard for that instrument must be low indeed, or he must feel that its 'provisions' ought not to be allowed to the people thereof. Hear what another leading republican says. W. O. Duval (let his name go down to posterity, together with his opinions and wishes!) writes thus: — ' I sincerely hope a civil war may soon burst upon the country. I want to see American slavery abolished in my time. Then my most fervent prayer is that England, France, and Spain may take this slavery-accursed nation into their special consideration; and when the time arrives for the streets of the cities of this " land of the free and home of the brave " to run with blood to the horses' bridles, if the writer of this be living, there will be one heart to rejoice at the retributive justice of heaven.' I propose further to call the attention of the House to an extract from a speech of the senior member from Ohio (Mr. Giddings). I do this the more readily because that he asked this

House, a few days since, to pass a resolution calling upon the President to state the time and place, when and where, and the persons who had any purpose to interfere with the domestic institutions of the Southern States. He says, 'Sir, I would intimidate no one; but I tell you there is a spirit in the North which will set at defiance all the low and unworthy machinations of this Executive, and of the minions of its power. When the contest shall come, when the thunder shall roll, and the lightning flash; when the slaves shall rise in the South, when, in imitation of the Cuban bondmen, the Southern slaves of the South shall feel that they are men; when they feel the stirring emotions of immortality, and recognise the stirring truth that they are men, and entitled to the rights which God has bestowed upon them; when the slave shall feel that, and when masters shall turn pale and tremble, when their dwellings shall smoke, and dismay sit on each countenance, then, Sir, I do not say, " We will laugh at your calamity, and mock when your fear cometh," but I do say, when that time shall come, the lovers of our race will stand forth and exert the legitimate powers of this Government for freedom. We shall then have constitutional power to act for the good of our country, and do justice to the slave. " Then will we strike off the shackles from the limbs of the slaves." That will be a period when this Government will have power to act between slavery and freedom, and when it can make peace by giving freedom to the slaves.   And let me tell you, Mr. Speaker, that that time hastens, it is rolling forward.   The President is exerting a power that will hasten it, though not intended by him; I hail it as I do the approaching dawn of that political and moral millennium which I am well assured will come upon the world.'

" Next I read from a speech made in Boston by Mr. Burlingame, member of this House, and a leading Republican, whose voice was heard in the recent canvass far away from his New-England home, in the prairies of the north-west, as well, perhaps, as in the Keystone State, when no doubt he advocated the same doctrines herein contained and earnestly appealed to Northern men to adopt them as their standard of political orthodoxy, and who, I may say, has been selected by his constituents to a seat in the Thirty-fifth Congress.   He said: — ' If asked to state specially what he would do, he would answer: First, repeal that Nebraska Bill; second, repeal the Fugitive Slave Law; third, abolish slavery in the district of Columbia; fourth, abolish the *inter-slave trade;* next, he would declare that slavery should not spread to one inch of the territory of the Union; he would then put the Government actually and perpetually on the side of freedom; he would have judges who believe in a higher law, and an anti-slavery constitution, an anti-slavery Bible, an anti-slavery God. Having thus denationalised slavery, he would not menace it in the States where it exists, but would say to these States, "It is your local institution; hug it to your bosoms until it shall destroy you." This is the only condition of repose, and it must come to this; for so long as life dwelt in his bosom so long would he fight for liberty and against slavery; and he hoped the time would soon come when the sun should not rise on a master nor set on a slave.' After this speech was delivered the Hon. Henry Wilson, the present senator for Massachusetts, being called for, rose and said: — ' This is not the time nor the place for me to utter a word. You have listened to the eloquence of my young friend, and here to-night I indorse every word and sentiment he has uttered. In public or in private life, in majorities or minorities, at home or abroad, I intend to live and die with unrelenting hostility to slavery on my lips.' Such language needs no comment from me to explain that, in the hands of these men, all of whom

are shining lights in the Republican party, the institutions of the Southern States would be crushed
out and destroyed.   And I think that the President
has very properly and truly characterised the objects
of these men and their associates as being dangerous
and revolutionary.   At all events, the only construction which I can give these sentiments is, that
slavery everywhere must fall, and our only condition
of repose is to be when ' the sun shall not rise upon
a master, nor set upon a slave.' "

CHAP. VI.

THE REAL POINTS OF THE QUESTION.

IT is difficult to say what are the relative chances of success of the two parties, in the total absence of all data upon which a calculation of the extent and duration of the warfare must be based; but the complete failures of the two main points which were put forward as the confident expectation of the Federal Government—1. the overwhelming of Southern opposition by the crushing force of an immediate attack; 2. the starving out of the South — go far to diminish the impression that the weight of money and power lies so entirely on the North side, as was at first presumed; while the unanimity of resistance, and measures taken to organise and concentrate its action, give no mean estimate of the strength and resources which will be forthcoming in a struggle *pro aris et focis.* The purchase of the cotton crop of this year by the Government of the Confederate States, and the issue of their notes in lieu of cash, will relieve any immediate pressure on their internal money market; while there is every indication that the abundant harvest which may in all human probability be expected, precludes all fear of the necessity which would compel submission.

A London paper, the most independent as it is unquestionably the ablest of our press, has lately entered its protest against the argument which the North has been trying to force against our better judgment. "In the ungrammatical chaos of President Lincoln's message, only a few insignificant sentences appear to relate to his illegal enforcement of martial law, while he passes over in sublime silence his unauthorised recognition of revolutionary government in Virginia. It is time to discontinue the affectation of regarding the Confederate States as mere violators of law. No impartial politician has disputed the right of the Federal, or any other government, to reclaim seceding sections of their subjects *if it can.* The question whether it is expedient or morally justifiable, must depend on the circumstances arising out of each particular case."*

* There is extant a pamphlet, written by a very respectable but rather damaged spinster, whose millennium arguments I have not found necessary to notice, as she adheres strictly to the moral ground where I could not follow her, as elderly cærulean maidens both demand and deserve more delicate handling than the stern nature of this inquiry allows ; besides, I cannot disguise from myself that

The North has been concentrating wealth and cheap labour, thus strengthening its position as manufacturer for the Union, and paving the way for the export of a large surplus of manufactures, when the South and West shall have made further progress in supplying themselves. It has enjoyed the entire markets of the Union as a means, so to speak, of learning its trade. It has retained the whole carrying trade of the country for its shipping. It has received a bounty in high tariffs during its weakness, to defend it from importation; and it has gradually acquired strength in experience, capital, and skill. It had before it a most brilliant future,

most of it is in the style of what vulgar boys call "My eye and Betty Martin O." One of such ladies, peradventure the reverend prophetess herself, inasmuch as the only authority she condescends to quote is this very pamphlet, has written this month, in the "Cornhill Magazine," a short philosophical notice of the crisis, in which she assumes that the South had no provocation to secede, that the rules laid down and acted on by known and fixed governments are applicable to that shadowy constitution which is the basis of the union of the United States. Also, that the Northern States are the legal holders of the constitutional powers under such Union, therefore they are bound, morally and socially, to coerce the South into obedience — but concludes that it would be the height of folly to attempt it, as they could not possibly keep them if they succeeded; and the height of wickedness to persevere, as the frightful expenditure of treasure and blood necessary does not justify any such madness. I heartily concur.

but it has wantonly disturbed that future by encouraging the growth of a political party based wholly upon sectional aggression, a party which proposes no issues of statesmanship for the benefit of the whole country. It advances nothing of a domestic or foreign policy tending to national profit or protection, or to promote the general welfare in any way. It simply denounces the system of labour which has conferred such prosperity upon the North, as a "moral wrong." While it disavows any intention of interfering with servitude at the South, it encourages, in every possible way, all that tends to undermine it. It enters the common national dwelling, and scatters firebrands amid the most solemn protestation of harmless intentions. It claims the right to explode mines, without being answerable for the mischief that may result. If questioned as to the object of such conduct, it replies that it is one of its "inalienable rights" so to act, and that certain persons who have combustible materials have had the effrontery to express fears of the consequences, and therefore it is the more bound to persist. It is for such reasoning as this that the North has, for more than ten years, constantly allowed itself to be irritated by incendiary speakers

and writers, whose sole stock in trade is the un-
reasoning hate against the South that may be en-
gendered by long-continued irritating misrepresen-
tation.

From time to time in the history of the country,
the attempt has been made to acquire party strength
by stirring up slumbering passions, and these attempts have always been made under the cloak of
philanthropy. These attempts have generally failed,
but their repetition with greater violence, from time
to time, has warped the truth in relation to the real
position of the Federal Government in regard to the
blacks, until the doctrine has acquired strength,
that one species of property, recognised by the Federal constitution, is without protection on Federal
soil. Thus, in the speech of William H. Seward, in
the national Senate, on the 29th of February, laying
down the platform of the party of which he is the
chief, he remarked : —

"Our fathers authorised Congress to make all
needful rules and regulations concerning the ma-
nagement and disposition of the public lands, and
to admit new States. So the constitution, while it
does not disturb or affect the system of capital in
slaves existing in any State under its own laws,
does, at the same time, *recognise every human being*

when within any exclusive sphere of Federal jurisdiction, not as capital, but as a person."

The spirit of this is contradicted in the succeeding lines, which claim that Congress conferred slavery upon six States, and prohibited it in seven, in a part of which it had existed before the territory became the property of the Union. Since the only powers possessed by the constitution are those especially delegated to it, the exercise of the power on the part of Congress to " confer," involves that of " exclusion." If it has power over any subject at all, it has the affirmative as well as the negative.

At the time of the formation of the Federal constitution, the law of nations recognised lawful property in African slaves throughout the civilised world. In that country they had been so held in every part of it from its earliest settlement. No colony was without owners of black property, and none doubted the legality of the holding.

It was not surprising that the generous-hearted of our own statesmen should have adopted the seductive but untried theory, and hesitate about the rightfulness of " holding property in man." Nevertheless the fact of the property in negroes existed, and the constitution was framed in the recognition of it. It has since been attempted to dispute whether the constitution recognised the blacks as property or as persons only. The generally received opinion, when the constitution was adopted, was that it recognised blacks as " property " only. The ultra men of that day contended that the constitution regarded them as something more than property, raising them to the level of " moral persons." Gradually ultra men denied that they are property at all under the constitution. Mr. Seward and his party are of those who contend for the latter, thus reversing the judgment which was held by the men who made the constitution. If we go back to the highest contemporaneous authority, we find Mr. Jay in the " Federalist " states it as follows : —

" We must deny the fact, that slaves are considered merely as property, and in no respect whatever as persons. The true state of the case is that they partake of both these qualities, being considered by our laws in some respects as persons, and in other respects as property. In being compelled to labour, not for himself, but for a master; in being vendible by one master to another master; and in being subject at all times to be restrained in his liberty and chastised in his body by the capricious will of his owner, the slave may appear to be degraded from the human rank, and classed with those irrational animals which fall under the legal denomination of property. In being protected, on the other hand, in his life and in his limbs, against the violence of all others, even the master of his labour and his liberty; and in being punishable himself for all violence committed against others; the slave is no less evidently regarded by the law as a member of the society, not as a part of the irrational creation; as a moral person, not as a mere article of property. The Federal constitution, therefore, decides with great propriety on the care of our slaves, when it views them in the mixed character of persons and property. This is, in fact, their true character; it is the character bestowed on them by the laws under which they live, and it will not be disputed that these are the proper criterion."

The progress of aggression upon the South and Southern rights in property is thus very clear. The constitutional " property " view of the black position was not left to be a barren idea; but under this view of " property " in blacks, Congress proceeded to act. A law was passed March 2nd, 1807, of which the 9th and 10th sections provide in substance as follows : —

" That the captain of any vessel of more than forty tons burden, sailing coastwise from one port of the United States to another, having on board per-sons of colour, to be transported in order to be sold or disposed of as slaves, shall make out and sub-scribe duplicate manifests, describing those slaves, and shall, with the owner or master, swear that they are not held to service or labour contrary to any law of the United States, or of the State."

The 9th section goes on to provide that the collector shall thereupon grant a *permit* to the master, authorising him to transport these slaves to the port where they are to be unladen, and forfeits any vessel departing without the manifest.

Section 10th provides: — "That the master of every vessel having on board persons of colour, to sell or dispose of as slaves, shall, upon arriving at his port of destination, before *unloading* these persons, exhibit a copy of the manifest to the collector." And the penalty for a refusal by the master of a vessel, laden as aforesaid, to deliver the manifest to the collector, is fixed at $10,000.

The laws of the United States have thus lawfully placed the slave on board a vessel of the United States, — have provided in what manner he shall be lawfully embarked, — in what manner he shall be landed at the port of destination, — regulating the trade altogether in the manner of "property," and that on the high seas under the national flag.

The object of the law thus regulating the transportation of black property, had special reference to the safety of that property in positions where it might be imperilled, viz. on the high seas, out of the jurisdiction of the State, but under the national flag. The idea had, probably, not then been broached, that the property of American citizens could be imperilled on the soil of the common country, by persons who, having abandoned their own similar " property," might seek to destroy that of their neighbours.

We find, in a contemporaneous history, a debate which took place January 2nd, 1799, during the administration of John Adams, and which throws some light on the views of Northern legislators of that day upon the same subject. On the day mentioned, Mr. Warin, of Philadelphia, presented a petition, praying for " a revision of the laws of the United States relative to the slave trade; of the act relative to fugitives from justice; and for the adoption of such measures as should in due time emancipate the whole of their brethren from their disagreeable situation."

" Mr. Rutledge opposed the petition. ' The gentlemen,' said he, 'who formerly used to advocate liberty, have retreated from their post, and committed the important trust to the care of " black patriots ; " they tell the House they are in slavery ; — thank God they are. They say they are not represented ; — certainly they are not; and I trust the day will never arrive when the Congress of the United States will display a parti-coloured assembly. Too much of this new-fangled French philosophy of liberty and equality has found its way among the gentlemen of our plantations, for which nothing will do but liberty.'

" Harrison G. Otis, of Massachusetts, brought forward his usual eloquence on this occasion. He said that though he possessed no slaves, he saw no reason why others might not, and that the proprietors of them were the fittest persons, and not Congress, to regulate that species of property.

" Mr. Thatcher, to the surprise of many, differed from his countryman, and thought the petitions for black men deserved equal consideration with those for whites.

" Mr. Brown, of Rhode Island, argued that the petition was but the contrivance of a combination of Jacobins, who had troubled Congress for many years past, and he feared never would cease.

He begged, therefore, that the gentlemen who put the petition on the table, might be desired to take it back again. He was truly sorry to see such a dangerous paper supported by such a worthy member of the House, and good Federalist, as Mr. Thatcher."

This incident is curious, since it shows that the " Black Patriots " of 1799, a " combination of Jacobins," who " never would cease troubling Congress," are the Black Republicans of the present day, still troubling it. While Mr. Thatcher, " a good Federalist," was the only one advocating the " troubling," Mr. Harrison Gray Otis referred the " property " to its "proprietors." The " Federalist " party, of which Mr. Thatcher was a " good one," also passed, in the Massachusetts Legislature, the resolution to " dissolve the Union," if Louisiana should be annexed. That party has " dissolved " on the occasion of every new slave State added to the Union since the annexation, no matter what " name " the party may have assumed for the moment. The free territory question has ever been revived when it was thought useful to defeat " the Democrats," which seems to have been its leading principle on all occasions, and at the present moment its " sole " principle.

John Adams was a shoemaker in Braintree, Massachusetts. When out of his time he studied law, on the advice of his uncle, a schoolmaster. He became, after the revolution, the leader of the Monarchical party, and his leading idea was "hereditary rulers;" and through his influence the alien and seditious laws were enacted. The former gave the executive absolute power over foreigners who arrived, and they were imprisoned and expelled for no reason but the will of the executive. The law of Congress in relation to the importation of such persons as any other States chose to admit, until 1808, was held to apply only to negroes; hence the alien law, originated by that founder of the party, now known as the Black Republican party, was allowed to operate against whites.

In a moral and religious view, slavery is indefensible; but I defy any one, whether European or American, to deny that it is not only allowed by the law of the United States, but guaranteed and protected by the most solemn forms of the Legislature. While the constitution was forming, and indeed long after, slavery was the rule in almost the whole of the nation. By degrees the Northern States found that their climate and land would pay better by other labour than negroes; the abolished the importation from Africa, and made a good bargain with the South for the sale of their slaves. By and by they proposed to the Southern States that they should do the same, but with this difference, that they should not be paid for getting rid of their slaves, and alleged that their land would be worth more by the change. The South replied that they were the best judges both of their convenience and their pockets, and that the law of the land protected their property. To this the Northerners answered that their productions of rice, tobacco, and cotton, were a commercial mistake, if not much overrated; and as to the law, their consciences would not allow them to be bound by such a law; and as an argument for the first proposition, instanced the amazing progress of wealth and prosperity in the non-slaveholding section of the Republic. The Southerners replied that such prosperity was the natural result of the trading and carrying monopoly, export and import from and to a country of such immense natural resources as the South, which had been secured to the North by a long series of prohibitory laws and tariffs; and moreover, that the well-known and avowed inclinations of the Southerners to establish free trade with the world, to break through these fetters and open their ports and commerce to foreign nations, are not an unlikely solution of the qualms of conscience in the second proposition.

The original pact of the United States of America provided for each separate State a *quasi* sovereignty, which included all the absolute rights of internal self-government, legislative and executive; the general body of the separate States agreeing to a Union, with a President governing by Senate and Congress, both nominated by the State Legislatures, and the supreme law administered by a Court of Judicature, appointed by the President for life.   The only act which gives power to the Government to repress by armed force resistance against its action was passed in 1795, by Congress, upon the occasion of insurrection in Pennsylvania, on account of riots consequent on the enforcing of some laws relating to whisky, &c., and applies solely to *insurrection*.   There is no statute existing which gives the Government a right to act by arms, except as against *insurrection*.   The action of the Supreme Court of Judicature has been frequently interrupted.   Although it is, by the constitution, the supreme law of the land, its decisions have been frequently disregarded with impunity; such as occurred when fourteen of the Northern State Legislatures passed acts in direct contravention of the judgment of the Supreme Court in the Dred-Scott case, besides individual instances in Pennsylvania and other places, in 1852, where the warrant of the Federal marshals, acting under the Supreme Court, was successfully resisted. It follows, therefore, that there does not exist such a polity in the United States as to give the Government an absolute legislative and executive control over the whole people, except by their express consent in the State Legislature enacted, but that its action in each State depends on the legal consent of the constituted authority in each separately. Now, right or wrong, the right of slave-holding has been the law of the United States of America, and its necessary consequences have been upheld by the successive Governments and the Supreme Court until 1860. The election of Abraham Lincoln entirely by the Northern States, without one single electoral vote in any Southern State, changed this order of things. The balance of might was by this thrown into the scale opposing the rights of the slave-owners, and immediately, as a necessary consequence, arose the secession. Now, it would be useless to argue the morality, as it would the question of force; we have only the plain constitutional bearing to look at. It is plainly competent for any individual State to retire from the Union by an act contemplated in the original compact which constituted such Union, and by no such act can resistance against the action of the Federal Government be construed into insurrection so as to justify the use of armed force by the Government. The secession, therefore, of the Southern States by the deliberate act of their legal authority cannot be called a rebellion; because, firstly, it is the exercise of a power reserved by the original compact of the Union; and, secondly, because the Government against which they are presumed to rebel has not the constitutional right of controlling their action. In fact, the opposition against the Federal Government has been, up to 1860, all on the side of the Northern States, when their rights were boldly and ably argued, and the question conceded, viz. that they had a right to separate if they wished it, and legally exercised that right—witness the public burning of the United States Constitution on the 4th of July in Massachusetts, &c., by Garrison, who was never indicted for treason. This being the position, that, the right of secession existing and having been acted upon legally, war between the Government and the seceding States is not a war of rebellion, as recognised by European history, but is more like the civil wars of the Italian republics in the fifteenth century, and solely depends on the *lex fortioris* for its justification. For the Federal Government have made no charge against the seceding States; they have issued no declaration, and published no manifesto, but simply an irregular and as it were tumultuous intention to co-erce ; whereas the Southern states have declared in the face of the world the grounds of their secession, the rights under which they act, and their mode of exercising them. What, then, should be the action of the governments of Europe? We have only to recognise powers that be. The sovereignty of the seceding States exists ; they are in absolute possession of their own land and their own Government, and this under an indefeasible constitutional right. What pretence, therefore, can any European government have for not recognising them as an independent sovereign power?

Such an antagonism, if ever carried into practical effect, must naturally induce coercion of the weaker section by the stronger, and if persisted in, must inevitably lead to disruption of the Union. This view was taken by every leading statesman without exception for the last thirty years, as we have seen in a former chapter. The usual consequences have been foreseen. In a leading London paper, the correspondent writes :—

" I have said that the great danger to the liberties of this country, and to the stability of its Government, is *not* from the rebels, but from the army. I shall be most happy, in the year 1862, if I can say that my prediction in regard to the army was false : but I am afraid it will not be. The army is the Congress of the United States. If General Scott should decide to be emperor after he has wiped out Jef. Davis, he might take the title of Emperor of Manhattan."

And is this to be the result of all the aspirations which guided the fathers of the American Commonwealth ?

The same amount of error which has apparently pervaded our contemporaries on this exciting question from the commencement of the difficulties in America, seems destined to overhang the public mind with its dark shadow until the natural and inevitable course of things dispels it. Up to the period of the taking of Fort Sumpter, an occurrence which might have been foreseen with certainty, it was insisted in this country that the quarrel would subside ; that our transatlantic cousins were too sensible to fight, and that the whole affair would find its termination in a " caucus " and a compromise. We are told that we must accept as unmistakeable the patriotic enthusiasm of the North, and recognise as genuine the great display of military strength of which it makes a boast. We are given to understand that the whole of the Northern States are of one

single mind, and are directing their full energies to
the suppression of an unnatural " rebellion," alike
insulting to the majesty of the Union, and despic-
able for its want of strength.   We are desired to
believe that the submission of the South is certain,
and probably nigh at hand, and that the discourage-
ment which prevails there is only to be equalled by
the glad anticipations of a victorious career in which
the Northern States indulge.   The liberality of the
loans — the great gathering of the citizens — the
vigour of the Government — the ardour of the
troops — are each and all pointed out to us as conclusive signs of the approaching quelling of an un-
healthy and unjustifiable revolt.   If we thought the
North entirely in the right, and the South entirely
in the wrong, we should be glad enough to recognise the correctness of this picture; but as it is our
opinion that the controversy can be fairly argued on
both sides, we do not affect to feel the interest we
are called upon to take in the seeming blazing patriotism of the North.   In the first place, then,
there is nothing more absurd than the idea of one
self-governed people trying to coerce another self-
ruled people into submission to its dictates.   There
is no political or social constitution in existence, or

which could ever be set on foot, that could establish on a firm foundation an anomaly like that. How much of truth may lie in the statements that have appeared as from respectable authority, that the " whole people of the United States are Sovereign," and that the " States " are mere subordinations, we will not undertake to say; but push the doctrine to its proper limits, and you dispose at once of the so-called independence of the States, in every possible respect. There would, under this theory, exist no more authority in their separate governments to enact State laws, than to settle principles for the intercourse of the Union even with foreign nations; and they would, in fact, be no more in the great Republic than the counties and parishes are in England. Granted, that at the time of the formation of the Union, the several States which joined it did so with no *animus revertendi*, that does not prevent their retaining the just right of seceding from the Union, if they find that their State interests are sacrificed.

But there is much more that may be said upon the question. It must not be forgotten that the North is hypocritical in the question of the "domestic institution." It is simply false to say that the North has been opposed to it, for without the commercial patronage which the North has given it, it would long ago have died a natural death.

Had not the merchants, and the bankers, and the brokers and shipowners of the North, fostered the trade in cotton, rice, and tobacco, in every possible way, it would have been impossible for the South to have maintained its slaves, and to have imparted the increase it has to that abominable system.

The "virtuous indignation" of the North at the present time, therefore, is an organised hypocrisy, and we can feel no interest in the so-called patriotic enthusiasm which the conflict is calling forth.

What are we to think of such prophecies as these? The rebellion will be put down before three weeks are over. It had its back broken long ago. It lacks every element of success. It has no money — no real honest troops—no backbone. In every Southern State an immense population stand ready to rise up for the Union. In a few days, in spite of tailor generals, the army will be in Richmond. The Union people of that city will illuminate it, when the troops arrive, for joy. In a few days the Union Legislature and provisional governor will be in Richmond, and rebellion will be squelched out. The nation will be *united.* There will be no disunion, no separation ; money will flow like water ; thousands of our wealthy people, and of our poor people, are commencing to bring out their household gods of gold and silver, and to melt them up to take a share in the United States loan. Every dollar will be taken up. It will be spent among ourselves at first, but England will get her share ere long.

But further — is this enthusiasm all real? Is the North entirely of one mind? Are all the citizens of the Northern States for abolition, or only some? Would they, or would they not, accept a compromise? And when they talk of putting down the " rebellion," would they not be ready to meet the Southern views if allowed to keep their Governmental places? We are satisfied they would; and that all this patriotic ebullition would give way before an arrangement that would satisfy and gratify that most worshipful of Yankee gods, the great almighty dollar.

Not so, however, with the South. The South is unmistakeably in earnest in this quarrel, and if it cannot boast of equal numbers, and equal wealth, to bring into the contest, it can rest upon entire union, and on the proud contempt in which it really holds the North. This fact has been most ably shown by the distinguished and unerring correspondent of our leading morning journal, who points out, in the clearest manner, the uncontrollable antipathy which exists in the Southern States against anything and everything connected with the North. Now, what else can arise from the undoubted state of things we have endeavoured to portray but a long and internecine conflict, in which *neither* side can be victorious? It is impossible to believe in what is called the " conquest of the South," or the " suppression " of the " rebellion "— it is impossible to understand what the North can really gain by an onslaught on the Southern States; and, as to renewal of the Union— as to a reconciliation of the Government as a political federation, it is and must be the merest dream, as long as four millions of Helots live — a standing controversy to disturb its peace.

CHAP. VII.

THE PRESENT POSITION OF AFFAIRS.

IT is positively distressing to read the pitiable rubbish which, disregarding all past experience, the papers daily produce as from correspondents over the water. The only man who has given us any views of his own, Mr. Russell, has also treated us to the headings of some of the veracious news published by these same gentry, for the information of the public there. It reminds us of the Neapolitan telegrams at the time of Garibaldi's expedition, when, out of 150 received in this country from Naples on the events of the day, 142 turned out to be wholly without foundation. The most audacious of these is undoubtedly Manhattan, whom I strongly suspect I know as the London correspondent of that precious Horace Greely, whose pious hopes and anticipations I have noticed above at p. 100.

It is clear the address to his letters of New York is not genuine, for in a late one he says, " I found the steamer had left the pier when I brought your parcel down, but I fortunately overtook her, and got it on board over the side, so that it was the last thing taken before she left the American shores." Did Manhattan foresee all this when he wrote the letter in New York; or did the parcel, so happily chucked on board, reach him in this good city, where he made up the farrago his friends had sent him? This Manhattan writes, almost daily, a letter to the " Standard," full of assertions, inferences, and opinions, which the leading articles of that ably conducted journal as invariably knock to pieces, on the principle, I suppose, of *audi alteram partem*, and certainly the *pars* taken is most undeniably *altera.* And no wonder, for he began by assuring us in the true style so well known and appreciated here, that " three weeks would see the Federal flag float over Richmond," when he proposed " to hang President Davis and all his rebel crew," and then, save the mark! " amid the acclamations of the Southern people, emancipated by such fraternal hands from the demagogues who had overridden them, proclaim the glorious Union undivided and indissoluble." Unfortunately, as in the Irishman's history, " those abominable facts " came in the way, and Manhattan's powers of prophecy were scattered to the four winds by the result of Scampers' Day, at Bulls Run.   But Manhattan was no ways abashed, not he, honest man.   " The Federal army fought splendidly, they fought like tigers, they were victorious ! "—oh, fie !— " but they were betrayed by imbecile generals, &c., &c., &c., and so they ran away."   Again, his figures have been rather oscillating for some days, but he seems to have at last settled down tolerably to 100,000 troops, in or near the field of battle, and about 400 killed, and 400 wounded.   A precious army it must have been to run, on suffering so unheard of a per-centage of loss !   Again, he ventures to sneer at the pusillanimity of the Confederate generals, at not improving their victory by marching straight on Washington.   He knows as well as I do, that the Federal army fought with Sharp's rifles, Colt's revolvers, and rifled cannon ; of all which munitions of war the Confederates were wholly in want.   And the veriest tyro in military matters would see the absurdity of leaving a strong fortified position with undisciplined troops, to take up an open position, where the rail would bring in converging lines the whole Northern population upon them. General Beauregard knows his business better.

He picked up a good deal he wanted, much more than the slaughter of these gallant invaders—which they threw away without stint,—arms, baggage, and cannon; those field-pieces which were the boast and pride of the New Yorkers. Alas! for the vanity of human aspirations. He even goes on to say Davis the rebel could have been the head of a strong military government, that the Northern States are so yearning for a King Stork for those loud croakers. "If," says Manhattan, "he had known he was victor, and followed our scared soldiers to Washington" (upon my word, Jeff. Davis ought to be very much obliged to him for the hint), "he could have taken Philadelphia and New York; so great and universal was the panic, that he could have even plundered Wall Street, and laid the city in ashes; and then nine-tenths of the people holding to the democratic doctrine 'to the victors belong the spoils,' he would have been allowed the Presidency he would have so gallantly won." What an exuberant imagination all this evidences; why, it beats the Richmond prophecy hollow! However, his imagination leads him into a most shameless and heartless fabrication, that the Confederates "cut the throats of the wounded, and also cut off, as trophies, noses, ears, and lips." In the name of common humanity let this horrible accusation be probed to the bottom.

In England we had the courage to sift the same terrible charge against the Sepoy fiends in the Mutiny, and though I remember *one case* fairly, if not quite, authenticated, I never heard of more. Can it then be true that Southern members of a common stock would so treat their fellow brethren? Manhattan must answer for this. But, after all, it is not worth one's while to sully one's hands with such people. Let us look at the position of affairs as they stand. Western Virginia is still occupied by a strong force, which, however, has retreated to Harper's Ferry. The centre of the frontier line is Columbia, with Washington as its quasi citadel. On the right of the Confederate forces is Fort Munroe, with a strong garrison under General Butler. It is clear therefore, that, unless he can detach sufficient bodies to rout the armies on his two flanks, General Beauregard cannot advance safely from his fortified lines. He has everything to gain by time. Some gentleman wrote in the *Times* " that drunkenness and insubordination prevailed to a fearful extent among the demoralised Federal army, but that *a few days* would see all rectified. They must have a receipt in those parts which the Iron Duke and Sir John Moore, and a hundred others, would have given something to know, when they had to reorganise a broken and retreating body. Beauregard has got to drill his troops, clothe them, arm them; and he means to do it effectually. What chances are there of the gallant Seward and Co., whose names now stink in the nostrils of their quondam friends, being able to force him into a successful engagement before he is ready? On land and sea they are spending nearer three million dollars a day than two. Their generals, who bloomed so suddenly from senators into brigadiers-general, have gone like the potatoes. I do not hear of any great anxiety to take up their loan. Sure I am, John Bull will certainly resent an attack on his pocket. He has suffered enough already, as George Colman sang :—

> Once to be done his anger did not touch,
>   But when a second time they tried the treason,
>   It made him crusty, sir, and with good reason ;
> You would be crusty were you *done too much.*

Nor do I think much of the tremendous offers of more troops, who march away the morning of battle because " their time was up ; " or if they stayed, and their time was not up, in another sense of the word, ran like the gallant Captain T. F. Meagher of the Sword did at the battle of the cabbages, immortalised by Thackeray in his " Three Pore Waits." It was reserved for Northern America to furnish the first instance of an army organised, we presume, to defend their country, imitating the conduct of a servant whose hiring was out, refusing to assist his master in putting out a fire in the house he had lived in. Why, the Free Lances of Italy, ruffians and bandits as they were, would have scorned such special pleading. They might have demanded every stiver of their pay before they drew their swords, and would have got it, too; but to sneak along the road home, while the ranks of their comrades were being mowed down within hearing, would have been too much for their stomach. No, depend upon it, the Northerners would not like to put their hands into the lobster's claw a second time in a hurry; and as the Southerners have always disavowed any intention of invading the North, as earnestly as they have sworn to exterminate an army that desecrates their own soil, Beauregard is not likely to give them a chance without due preparation.

In the meantime quiet people are murmuring What is to be the end of all this? and, like most good people, are swamped by a surging, angry mob, who, when they find all the destruction of their magnificent trade by this detestable warfare comes down upon their own pockets,—" *postquam cerdonibus esse timendus cœperit* " — will have something to say to the authors of their misery.

Separation is final and irrevocable. There can be no faith between the contracting parties to any scheme of reconciliation between the Northern and Southern sections of the defunct United States. A glorious career is open to both. No one can deny the highest meed of enterprise, intelligence, and daring to the hardy Northerners, and the immense advantages which free trade offers to the universal world in the illimitable resources of their country, now for the first time open to foreigners, must advance the less enterprising but more polished Southerner in the race of civilisation. We in England trust its first fruits will be seen in the amelioration of the condition of their slaves. Their own interest, their own sound and good common sense, when not outraged by coercion or insulted by insidious advice and the denunciations of pious charlatans, will lead them themselves to consider how they can best set about modifying an evil most of them cannot honestly deny that they deplore.

Let them once be called into the noble family of nations. Let them stand forth the equals and brethren of all the Anglo-Saxon race throughout the world, and we do not despair of seeing them fulfil a glorious destiny.

We heartily wish them God speed.

APPENDICES.

APPENDIX I.

President Lincoln's Inaugural Address, Delivered March 4th, 1861.

" FELLOW-CITIZENS OF THE UNITED STATES : —

" In compliance with a custom as old as the Government itself, I appear before you to address you briefly, and to take in your presence the oath prescribed by the Constitution of the United States to be taken by the President before he enters on the execution of his office.

" I do not consider it necessary at present for me to discuss those matters of administration about which there is no special anxiety or excitement.

" Apprehension seems to exist among the people of the Southern States that, by the accession of a Republican Administration, their property and their peace, and personal security are to be endangered. There has never been any reasonable cause for such apprehension. Indeed, the most ample evidence to the contrary has all the while existed and been open to their inspection. It is found in nearly all the public speeches of him who now addresses you. I do but quote from one of those speeches when I declare that 'I have no purpose, directly or indirectly, to interfere with the institution of slavery in the States where it exists; I believe I have no lawful right to do so, and I have no inclination to do so.' Those who nominated and elected me did so with a full knowledge that I had made this and many similar declarations, and had never recanted them. And more than this, they placed in the platform for my acceptance, and as a law to themselves and to me, the clear and emphatic Resolution which I now read:—

"'*Resolved*, That the maintenance inviolate of the rights of the States, and especially the right of each State to order and control its own domestic institutions according to its own judgment exclusively, is essential to that balance of power on which the perfection and endurance of our political fabric depend, and we denounce the lawless invasion by armed force of the soil of any State or territory, no matter under what pretext, as the gravest of crimes.'

"I now reiterate these sentiments, and in doing so I only press upon the public attention the most conclusive evidence of which the case is susceptible, that the property, peace, and security of no section are to be in anywise endangered by the now incoming Administration. I add, too, that all the protection which, consistently with the Constitution and the laws, can be given, will be cheerfully given to all the States, when lawfully demanded, for whatever cause, as cheerfully to one section as to another.

" There is much controversy about the delivering up of fugitives from service or labour. The clause I now read is as plainly written in the Constitution as any other of its provisions : —

"' No person held to service or labour in one State, under the laws thereof, escaping into another, shall, in consequence of any law or regulation therein, be discharged from such service or labour, but shall be delivered up on claim of the party to whom such service or labour may be due.'

"It is scarcely questioned that this provision was intended by those who made it for the reclaiming of what we call fugitive slaves; and the intention of the lawgiver is the law. All members of Congress swear their support to the whole Constitution, to this provision as much as any other. To the proposition, then, that slaves, whose cases come within the terms of this clause, 'shall be delivered up,' their oaths are unanimous. Now, if they would make the effort in good temper, could they not, with nearly equal unanimity, frame and pass a law by means of which to keep good that unanimous oath? There is some difference of opinion whether this clause should be enforced by national or by State authority; but surely that difference is not a very material one. If the slave is to be surrendered, it can be of but little consequence to him or to others by which authority it is done. And should any one, in any case, be content that this oath shall go unkept on a merely unsubstantial controversy as to how it shall be kept? Again, in any law upon this subject, ought not all the safeguards of liberty known in civilised and humane jurisprudence to be introduced, so that a free man be not, in any case surrendered as a slave? And might it not be well at the same time to provide by law for the enforcement of that clause in the Constitution which guarantees that 'the citizens of each State shall be entitled to all the privileges and immunities of citizens in the several States?' I take the official oath to-day with no mental reservations, and with no purpose to construe the Constitution or laws by any hypercritical rules; and while I do not choose now to specify particular Acts of Congress as proper to be enforced, I do suggest that it will be much safer for all, both in official and private stations, to conform to and abide by all those Acts which stand unrepealed, than to violate any of them, trusting to find impunity in having them held to be unconstitutional.

"It is seventy-two years since the first inauguration of a President under our National Constitution. During that period fifteen different and greatly distinguished citizens have in succession administered the executive branch of Government. They have conducted it through many perils, and generally with great success. Yet, with all this scope for precedent, I now enter upon the same task, for the brief constitutional term of four years, under great and peculiar difficulty. A disruption of the Federal Union, heretofore only menaced, is now formidably attempted. I hold that, in contemplation of universal law and of the Constitution, the Union of these

States is perpetual. Perpetuity is implied, if not expressed, in the fundamental law of all national governments. It is safe to assert that Government proper never had a provision in its organic law for its own termination. Continue to execute all the express provisions of our National Constitution, and the Union will endure for ever, it being impossible to destroy it except by some action not provided for in the instrument itself. Again, if the United States be not a Government proper, but an association of States in the nature of a contract merely, can it as a contract be peaceably unmade by less than all the parties who made it? One party to a contract may violate it—break it, so to speak—but does it not require all to lawfully rescind it?

" Descending from these general principles, we find the proposition that, in legal contemplation, the Union is perpetual, confirmed by the history of the Union itself.

"The Union is much older than the Constitution. It was formed, in fact, by the Articles of Association in 1744. It was matured and continued in the Declaration of Independence in 1776. It was further matured, and the faith of all the then thirteen States expressly plighted and engaged that it should be perpetual, by the Articles of Confederation in 1778; and finally, in 1787, one of the declared objects for ordaining and establishing the Constitution was to form a more perfect Union. But if the destruction of the Union by one or by a part only of the States be lawfully possible, the Union is less than before, the Constitution having lost the vital element of perpetuity.

"It follows from these views that no State, upon its own mere motion, can lawfully get out of the Union; that resolves and ordinances to that effect are legally void, and that acts of violence within any State or States against the authority of the United States, are insurrectionary or revolutionary, according to circumstances. I therefore consider that, in view of the Constitution and the laws, the Union is unbroken, and to the extent of my ability I shall take care, as the Constitution itself expressly enjoins upon me, that the laws of the Union be faithfully executed in all the States. Doing this I deem to be only a simple duty on my part. I shall perfectly perform it, so far as is practicable, unless my rightful masters, the American people, shall withhold the requisition, or in some authoritative manner direct the contrary. I trust this will not be regarded as a menace, but only as the declared purpose of the Union, that it will constitutionally defend and maintain itself.

"In doing this, there need be no bloodshed or violence, and there shall be none, unless it is forced upon the national authority. The power confided to me will be used, to hold, occupy, and possess the property and places belonging to the Government, and collect the duties and imposts; but beyond what may be necessary for these objects, there will be no invasion—no using of force against or amongst the people anywhere.

"Where hostility to the United States shall be so great and so universal as to prevent competent resident citizens from holding the Federal offices, there will be no attempt to force obnoxious strangers among the people that object. While the strict legal right may exist of the Government to enforce the exercise of these offices, the attempt to do so would be so irritating and so nearly impracticable withal that I deem it better. to forego for the time the usage of such offices.

" The mails, unless repelled, will continue to be furnished in all parts of the Union.

So far as possible, the people everywhere shall have that sense of perfect security which is most favourable to calm thought and reflection. The course here indicated will be followed, unless current events and experience shall show a modification or change to be proper ; and in every case and exigency my best discretion will be exercised according to the circumstances actually existing, and with a view and a hope of a peaceful solution of the national troubles and the restoration of fraternal sympathies and affections. That there are. persons in one section or another who seek to destroy the Union at all events, and are glad of any pretext to do it, I will neither affirm nor deny. But if there be such, I need address no word to them.

" To those, however, who really love the Union, may I not speak ? Before entering upon so grave a matter as the destruction of our national fabric, with all its benefits, its memories, and its hopes, would it not be well to ascertain why we do it ? Will you hazard so desperate a step while there is any portion of the ills you fly from that have no real existence ? Will you, while the certain ills you fly to are greater than all the real ones you fly from? Will you risk the commission of so fearful a mistake? All profess to be content in the Union if all constitutional rights can be maintained. Is it true, then, that any right, plainly written in the Constitution, has been denied? I think not. Happily the human mind is so constituted that no party can reach to the audacity of doing this. Think, if you can, of a single instance in which a plainly written provision of the Constitution has ever been denied. If, by the mere force of numbers, a majority should deprive a minority of any clearly-written constitutional right, it might in a moral point of view, justify revolution; certainly would, if such right were a vital one. But such is not the case.

"All the vital rights of minorities and of individuals are so plainly assured to them by affirmations and negations, guarantees and prohibitions, in the Constitution, that controversies never arise concerning them. But no organic law can ever be framed with a provision specially applicable to every question which may occur in practical administration. No foresight can anticipate, nor any document of reasonable length contain, express provisions for all possible questions. Shall fugitives from labour be surrendered by National or by State authority? The Constitution does not expressly say. Must Congress protect slavery in the territories? The Constitution does not expressly say. From questions of this class spring all our constitutional controversies, and we divide upon them into majorities and minorities.

"If the minority will not acquiesce, the majority must,

or the Government must cease. There is no alternative for continuing the Government but acquiescence on the one side or the other. If a minority in such a case will secede rather than acquiesce, they make a precedent which in turn will ruin and divide them, for a minority of their own will secede from them whenever a majority refuses to be controlled by such a minority. For instance, why not any portion of a new Confederacy, a year or two hence, arbitarily secede again, precisely as some portions of the present Union now claim to secede from it? All who cherish disunion sentiments are now being educated to the exact temper of doing this. Is there such perfect identity of interests among the States to comprise a new Union as to produce harmony only and prevent renewed secession? Plainly, the central idea of secession is the essence of anarchy.

"A majority held in restraint by constitutional checks and limitations, and always changing easily, with deliberate changes of popular opinions and sentiments, is the only true sovereign of a free people. Whoever rejects it does, of necessity, fly to anarchy or to despotism. Unanimity is impossible. The rule of a minority, as a permanent arrangement, is wholly inadmissible. So that, rejecting the majority principle, anarchy or despotism in some form is all that is left.

"I do not forget the position assumed by some, that constitutional questions are to be decided by the Supreme Court, nor do I deny that such decisions must be binding, in any case, upon the parties to a suit, as to the object of that suit, while they are also entitled to very high respect and consideration in all parallel cases by all other departments of the Government; and while it is obviously possible that such decision may be erroneous in any given case, still the evil effect following it, being limited to that particular case, with the chance that it may be overruled and never become a precedent for other cases, can better be borne than could the evils of a different practice. At the same time, the candid citizen must confess that if the policy of the Government upon the vital questions affecting the whole people, is to be irrevocably fixed by the decisions of the Supreme Court, the instant they are made in ordinary litigation between parties in personal actions, the people will have ceased to be their own masters, having to that extent practically resigned their Government into the hands of that eminent tribunal. Nor is there in this view any assault upon the court or the judges.

"It is a duty from which they may not shrink to decide cases properly brought before them, and it is no fault of theirs if others seek to turn their decisions to political purposes. One section of our country believes slavery is right, and ought to be extended, while the other believes it is wrong, and ought not to be extended. This is the only substantial dispute; and the fugitive slave clause of the Constitution, and the law for the suppression of the foreign slave trade, are each as well enforced, perhaps, as any law can ever be in a community where the moral sense of the people imperfectly supports the law itself. The great body of the people abide by the dry, legal obligations in both cases, and a

few break over in each. This, I think, cannot be perfectly cured, and it would be worse in both cases, after
the separation of the sections than before. The foreign
slave trade, now imperfectly suppressed, would be
ultimately revived, without restriction in one section,
while fugitive slaves, now only partially surrendered,
would not be surrendered at all by the other. Physically
speaking, we cannot separate—we cannot remove our
respective sections from each other, nor build an impassable wall between them. A husband and wife may be
divorced and go out of the presence and beyond the
reach of each other; but the different parts of our
country cannot do this. They cannot but remain face
to face, and intercourse, either amicable or hostile, must
continue between them. Is it possible, then, to make
that intercourse more advantageous or more satisfactory
after separation than before? Can aliens make treaties
easier than friends can make laws? Can treaties be
more faithfully enforced between aliens than laws can
among friends? Suppose you go to war; you cannot
fight always, and when, after much loss on both sides
and no gain on either, you cease fighting, the identical
questions as to terms of intercourse are again upon you.
This country, with its institutions, belongs to the people
who inhabit it. Whenever they shall grow weary of the
existing Government, they can exercise their constitutional right of amending, or their revolutionary right to
dismember or overthrow it. I cannot be ignorant of
the fact that many worthy and patriotic citizens are
desirous of having the National Constitution amended.

While I make no recommendation of amendment, I freely recognize the full authority of the people over the whole subject, to be exercised in either of the modes prescribed in the instrument itself; and I should, under existing circumstances, favour rather than oppose a fair opportunity being afforded the people to act upon it. I will venture to add that to me the Convention mode seems preferable, in that it allows amendments to originate with the people themselves, instead of only permitting them to take or reject propositions originated by others not specially chosen for the purpose, and which might not be precisely such as they would wish themselves to accept or refuse. I understand a proposed amendment to the Constitution—which amendment, however, I have not seen—has passed Congress, to the effect that the Federal Government shall never interfere with the domestic institutions of States, including that of persons held to service. To avoid misconstruction of most I have said, I depart from my purpose not to speak of particular amendments, so far as to say that, holding such a provision as now implied to be constitutional law, I have no objection to its being made express and irrevocable. The chief magistrate derives all his authority from the people, and they have conferred now upon him to fix the terms for the separation of the States. The people themselves also can do this if they choose, but the Executive, as such, has nothing to do with it. His duty is to administer the present Government as it came to his hands, and to transmit it unimpaired by him to his successor. Why should there not be a patient confidence in the ultimate justice of the people? Is there any better or equal hope in the world? In our present differences, is either party without faith of being in the right? If the Almighty Ruler of nations, with his eternal truth and justice, be on your side of the North, or on yours of the South, that truth and that justice will surely prevail by the judgment of this great tribunal—the American people. By the frame of the Government under which we live, this same people have wisely given their public servants but little power for mischief, and have, with equal wisdom, provided for the return of that little to their own hands at very short intervals. While the people retain their virtue and vigilance, no administration, by any extreme wickedness or folly, can very seriously injure the Government in the short space of four years.

" My countrymen, one and all, think calmly and well upon this whole subject. Nothing valuable can be lost by taking time.

" If there be an object to hurry any of you, in hot haste, to a step which you could never take deliberately, that object will be frustrated by taking time; but no good object can be frustrated by it. Such of you as are now dissatisfied still have the old Constitution unimpaired, and, on the sensitive point, the laws of your own framing under it, while the new Administration will have no immediate power, if it would, to change either. If it were admitted that you who are dissatisfied hold the right side in the dispute, there still is no single reason for precipitate action. Intelligence, patriotism, Christianity, and a firm reliance on Him who has never yet forsaken this favoured land, are still competent to adjust in the best way all our present difficulty.

"In your hands, my dissatisfied fellow-countrymen, and not in mine, is the momentous issue of civil war. The Government will not assail you. You can have no conflict without being yourselves the aggressors. You have no oath registered in heaven to destroy the Government, while I shall have the solemn one to 'preserve, protect, and defend' it. I am loth to close. We are not enemies, but friends. We must not be enemies. Though passion may have strained, it must not break our bonds of affection. The mystic chords of memory, stretching from every battle-field and patriotic grave to every living heart and hearthstone all over this broad land, will yet swell the chorus of the Union, when again touched, as surely they will be, by the better angels of our nature."

The first war proclamation was issued by the President as follows: —

" By the President of the United States.

" A Proclamation.

" Whereas the laws of the United States have been for some time past, and now are opposed, and the execution thereof obstructed, in the States of South Carolina,

Georgia, Alabama, Florida, Mississippi, Louisiana, and Texas, by combinations too powerful to be suppressed by the ordinary course of judicial proceedings, or by the powers vested in the marshals by law :

"Now, therefore, I, Abraham Lincoln, President of the United States, in virtue of the power in me vested by the Constitution and the laws, have thought fit to call forth, and hereby do call forth, the militia of the several States of the Union, to the aggregate number of 75,000, in order to suppress said combinations, and to cause the laws to be duly executed.

" The details for this object will be immediately communicated to the State authorities through the War Department. I appeal to all loyal citizens to favour, facilitate, and aid this effort to maintain the power, the integrity, and the existence of our national Union and the perpetuity of popular government, and to redress wrongs already long enough endured.

"I deem it proper to say that the first service assigned to the forces hereby called forth will probably be to repossess the forts, places, and property which have been seized from the Union; and in every event the utmost care will be observed, consistently with the objects aforesaid, to avoid any devastation, any destruction of, or interference with property, or any disturbance of peaceful citizens in any part of the country ; and I hereby command the persons composing the combinations aforesaid to disperse and retire peaceably to their respective abodes within twenty days from this date.

" Believing that the present condition of public affairs

presents an extraordinary occasion, I do hereby, in virtue of the power in me vested by the Constitution, convene both Houses of Congress. The senators and representatives are therefore summoned to assemble at their respective Chambers at twelve o'clock noon, on Thursday, the 4th day of July next, then and there to consider and determine such measures as, in their wisdom, the public safety and interest may seem to demand.

" In witness whereof, I have hereunto set my hand and caused the seal of the United States to be affixed.

" Done at the City of Washington this 15th day of April, in the year of our Lord 1861, and of the Independence of the United States the 85th.

" By the President,

" ABRAHAM LINCOLN.

" WILLIAM H. SEWARD, Secretary of State."

" Proclamation of the President of the Confederate States of America.

" WHEREAS, Abraham Lincoln, President of the United States, has, by proclamation, announced intention of invading the Confederacy with an armed force for the purpose of capturing its fortresses, and thereby subverting its independence and subjecting the free people thereof to the dominion of a foreign power; and whereas it has thus become the duty of this Government to repel the threatened invasion and defend the rights and liberties of the people by all the means which the laws of nations and usages of civilised warfare place at its disposal.

" Now, therefore, I, Jefferson Davis, President of the Confederate States of America, do issue this, my proclamation, inviting all those who may desire, by service in private armed vessels on the high seas, to aid this Government in resisting so wanton and wicked an aggression, to make application for commissions or letters of marque and reprisal, to be issued under the seal of these Confederate States; and I do further notify all persons applying for letters of marque, to make a statement in writing, giving the name and suitable description of the character, tonnage, and force of the vessel, name of the place of residence of each owner concerned therein, and the intended number of crew, and to sign each statement, and deliver the same to the Secretary of State or collector of the port of entry of these Confederate States, to be by him transmitted to the Secretary of State, and I do further notify all applicants aforesaid, before any commission or letter of marque is issued to any vessel, or the owner or the owners thereof, and the commander for the time being, they will be required to give bond to the Confederate States, with at least two responsible sureties not interested in such vessel, in the penal sum of five thousand dollars, or if such vessel be provided with more than one hundred and fifty men, then in the penal sum of ten thousand dollars, with the condition that the owners, officers, and crew who shall be employed on board such commissioned vessel shall observe the laws of these Confederate States, and the instructions given them for the regulation of their conduct, that shall satisfy all damages done contrary to the tenor thereof by such vessel during her commission, and deliver up the same when revoked by the President of the Confederate States. And I do further specially enjoin on all persons holding offices, civil and military, under the authority of the Confederate States, that they be vigilant and zealous in the discharge of the duties incident thereto; and I do, moreover, exhort the good people of these Confederate States, as they love their country—as they prize the blessings of free Government—as they feel the wrongs of the past, and those now threatened in an aggravated form by those whose enmity is more implacable, because unprovoked—they exert themselves in preserving order, in promoting concord, in maintaining the authority and efficacy of the laws, and in supporting, invigorating all the measures which may be adopted for a common defence, and by which, under the blessings of Divine Providence, we may hope for a speedy, just, and honourable peace.

"In witness whereof I have set my hand, and have caused the seal of the Confederate States of America to be attached, this 17th day of April, in the year of our Lord 1861.

"JEFFERSON DAVIS.

"ROBERT TOOMBS, Secretary of State."

APPENDIX II.

Report of the Joint Committee of the General Assembly of Virginia, January 26th, 1860, Doc. No. XXXI.

"The evidence before your committee is sufficient to show the existence, in a number of Northern States, of a wide-spread conspiracy, not merely against Virginia, but against the peace and security of all the Southern States. But the careful erasure of names and dates from many of the papers found in Brown's possession, renders it difficult to procure legal evidence of the guilt of the parties implicated. The conviction of the existence of such a conspiracy is deepened by the sympathy with the culprits which has been manifested by large numbers of persons in the Northern States, and by the disposition which your committee are satisfied did exist, to rescue them from the custody of the law.

" The subject of slavery has, from time to time, constituted a disturbing element in our political system, from the foundation of our confederated republic. At the date of the declaration of our national independence, slavery existed in every colony of the confederation. It had been introduced by the mother country, against the wishes and remonstrances of the colonies. It is true that in the more Northern members of the confederation the number of slaves was small ; but the institution was recognised and protected by the laws of all the colonies.

" Experience had shown that the African race were not adapted to high Northern latitudes, and that slave labour could not compete successfully with free white labour in those pursuits to which the industry of the North was directed. This discovery having been made, the people of the North, at an early day, began to dispose of their slaves, by sale, to citizens of the Southern States, whose soil, climate, and productions were better adapted to their habits and capacities ; and the legislation of the Northern States, following the course of public opinion, was directed not to emancipation, but to the removal of the slave population beyond their limits. To effect this object, they adopted a system of laws which provided, prospectively, that all children born of female slaves, within their jurisdiction, after certain specified dates, should be held free when they attained a given age. No law can be found on the statute book of any Northern State, which conferred the boon of freedom on a single slave in being. All who were slaves remained slaves.

" By these laws a wholesale slave trade was inaugurated, under which a large proportion of the slaves of the Northern States were sold to persons residing south of Pennsylvania ; and it is an unquestionable fact, that a large number of the slaves of the Southern States are the descendants of those sold by Northern men to citizens of the South, with covenants of general warranty of title to them and their increase.

"Chief Justice Parsons, in delivering the opinion of the Court in Winchedon *v.* Hatfield, 4 Mass. R. 127, says, 'Slavery was introduced into this country soon after its first settlement, and was tolerated until the ratification of the present Constitution (2nd March, 1780). The slave was the property of his master, subject to his orders, to reasonable correction for misbehaviour, was transferable like a chattel by gift or sale, and was assets in the hands of his executor or administrator. If the master was guilty of a cruel or unreasonable castigation of his slave, he was liable to be punished for a breach of the peace, and I believe the slave was allowed to demand sureties of the peace from a violent and barbarous master,—which generally caused a sale to another master. And the issue of the female slave, according to the maxim of the civil law, was the property of her master. Under these regulations, the treatment of slaves was in general mild and humane, and they suffered hardships not greater than hired servants.'

"As late as 1830 there were slaves in every New England State except Vermont.

"The first form in which the slavery question presented itself to the framers of the Constitution, was in regard to the relation of the slave population to taxation and representation. This question was adjusted without much debate, to the satisfaction of all parties, in conformity with the rule previously established in the Continental Congress, by a compromise, which stipulated that three-fifths of the slave population should be counted in establishing the ratio of representation, and in the imposition of direct taxes. The vote by States on this proposition stood: Ayes—Massachusetts, Connecticut, New York, Pennsylvania, Maryland, Virginia, North Carolina, South Carolina, and Georgia—9. Nays—New Jersey and Delaware—2. Elliott's Debates, vol. i. p. 203.

" The next aspect in which the subject arose was in regard to the suppression of the African slave trade; and here again the subject of difference was settled in a wise spirit of conciliation and mutual concession.

" The third and last form in which the subject of slavery was considered by the convention, was in reference to the surrender of fugitive slaves. The provision on this subject came up for consideration on the 29th of August, 1787. It was in these words : 'If any person be bound to service or labour in any part of the United States, and shall escape into another State, he or she shall not be discharged from such service or labour, in consequence of any regulation subsisting in the State to which they shall escape, but shall be delivered up to the person justly claiming their service or labour.'

" The propriety and justice of this provision were so obvious, that it was adopted by the unanimous vote of the convention.

" When their work was accomplished, by order of the convention, it was submitted to the Continental Congress, accompanied by a letter from George Washington, which is so replete with just and patriotic sentiments, and so instructive as to the motives by which the convention was guided, that your committee cannot forbear to make some extracts from it. This letter, addressed to his excellency, the President of Congress, was approved Sept. 17th, 1787, by unanimous order of the convention.

"'It is obviously impracticable,' writes this wisest and most patriotic of statesmen, 'in the Federal Government of these States, to secure all rights of independent sovereignty to each, and yet provide for the interest and safety of all. Individuals entering into society must give up a share of liberty to preserve the rest. The magnitude of the sacrifice must depend as well on situation and circumstances as on the object to be obtained. It is at all times difficult to draw, with precision, the line between those rights which must be surrendered and those which may be reserved ; and on the present occasion, this difficulty was increased by a difference among the several States as to their situation, extent, habits, and particular interests.

"'In all our deliberations on this subject, we kept steadily in our view that which appears to us the greatest interest of every true American — the consolidation of our Union — in which is involved our property, felicity, safety, perhaps our national existence. This important consideration, seriously and deeply impressed on our minds, led each State in the convention to be less rigid on points of inferior magnitude than might have been otherwise expected ; and thus the Constitution which we now present is the result of a spirit of amity, and of that mutual deference and concession which the peculiarity of our political situation rendered indispensable.

"'That it will meet the full and entire approbation of

every State, is not, perhaps to be expected; but each
will doubtless consider that, had her interest been alone
consulted, the consequences might have been particularly
disagreeable or injurious to others; that it is liable to
as few exceptions as could reasonably have been expected, we hope and believe; that it may promote the
lasting welfare of that country so dear to us all, and secure her freedom and happiness, is our most ardent wish.'

"It is doubtless true, that the Constitution was not,
in all its details, acceptable to a single State represented
in the convention. But it embodied the results of their
joint counsels, governed by a spirit of concord and
amity, in obedience to which each State agreed to make
some concessions for the common good.

"In 1802, the subject of the duty of the States under
the Federal Constitution was referred to in the Supreme
Court of Vermont, and the judges availed themselves of
the occasion to give expression to sentiments which deserve to be deeply impressed on the hearts of the people
of all sections. Judge Tyler remarked, 'With respect
to what has been observed on the Constitution and laws
of the Union, I will observe that whoever views atten·
tively the Constitution of the United States, while he
admires the wisdom which framed it, will perceive that
in order to unite the interests of a numerous people,
inhabiting a broad extent of territory, and possessing,
from education and habits, different modes of thinking
on important subjects, it was necessary to make numerous provisions in favour of local prejudices, and so to
construct the Constitution, and so to enact the laws made

under it, that the rights or supposed rights of all should be secured throughout the whole national domain. In compliance with the spirit of this Constitution, upon our admission into the Federal Union, the statute laws of this State were revised, and a penal act, which was supposed to militate against the third member of the second section of the 4th article of the Constitution of the United States, was repealed ; and if cases shall happen in which our local sentiments and feelings may be violated, yet I trust that the good people of Vermont will, on all such occasions, submit with cheerfulness to the national Constitution and laws, which, if we may wish, in some particular, more congenial to our modes of thinking, yet we must be sensible are productive of numerous and rich blessings to us as individuals, and to the State as an integral part of the Union.'

" Chief Justice Jonathan Robinson, spoke as follows : 'I concur fully in opinion with the Assistant Judge. I shall always respect the Constitution and laws of the Union; and though it may sometimes be a reluctant, yet I shall always render a prompt obedience to them, fully sensible that while I reverence a Constitution and laws which favour the opinions and prejudices of the citizens of other sections of the Union, the same Constitution and laws contain also provisions which are favourable to our peculiar opinions and prejudices, and which may possibly be equally irreconcilable with the sentiments of the inhabitants of other States, as the very idea of slavery is to us.' See 2 Tyler's Rep.199, 200.

" The acquisition of Louisiana and Florida, embracing

a large extent of territory adapted to slave labour, gave rise to some uneasiness in the Northern mind in regard to the future ascendancy of the slave States in the national councils. This uneasiness continued to increase until 1820, when it developed itself practically by an attempt to impose restrictions on the State of Missouri, as conditions precedent to her admission into the Union. It is but just, however, to state that the struggle on this question was marked not so much by hostility to slavery as by jealousy of the growing political power of the Southern States. The contest in regard to the terms on which Missouri should be admitted created deep feeling throughout the Union. It was the first occasion on which parties were arrayed according to geographical divisions, and it was at once perceived that a contest of that character was fraught with danger to the harmony and permanency of the Union. Fortunately, the restrictions on the State of Missouri were defeated. A line of partition was subsequently drawn through the unoccupied territory of the United States, along the parallel of 36° 30′ to our western frontier, with an enactment that slavery was to be prohibited in all the territory north of that line, and permitted, if desired by the people, in all south of it. By this arrangement the two systems of civilisation and labour were left to progress westward, side by side.

" Such was the aspect of the slavery question in 1843-4, when Texas, which had recently established her independence after a gallant struggle with Mexico, sought admission into our Union. There was great diversity of opinion among the people of the United States, both in the Northern and Southern States, as to the policy of receiving her into our confederacy. Animated discussions ensued in all parts of the country on this great question; and finally, so absorbing was the interest which was felt in it, that the question of admission or non-admission became an important element in the presidential election of 1844. James K. Polk was the representative of those favourable to admission, and Henry Clay of those opposed to it. On this great issue the parties went before the country, and the verdict of public opinion was in favour of the admission of Texas as a slave State, and with a stipulation in the form of an irrevocable compact, that, at a future day, four more slave States might be carved out of her vast territory, as the convenience of her advancing population might require. The Northern or non-slaveholding States which voted for Mr. Polk were Maine, New Hampshire, New York, Pennsylvania, Indiana, Illinois and Michigan, giving 103 electoral votes. The slave States voting with them were Virginia, South Carolina, Georgia, Alabama, Mississippi, Louisiana, Missouri and Arkansas—67 electoral votes.

" The admission of Texas was soon followed by the war with Mexico, which, after a series of brilliant victories, resulted in the subjugation of her capital, and the ratification of the treaty of Guadaloupe Hidalgo, by which she ceded to the United States Upper California, New Mexico, and other territory west of our ancient frontier. The *status* of these territories, in regard to slavery, was unsettled, and immediately after the ratification of the treaty of peace, an animated struggle on this question arose in the two branches of Congress.

"The South promptly proposed a compromise, by which the line of partition along the parallel of 36° 30′ should be extended to the Pacific Ocean, and that the covenants of the Missouri compromise should be extended to all the newly-acquired territory. This proposition was rejected by the North, and an angry contest ensued, which seriously endangered the peace and tranquillity of the Union. Peaceful counsels, however, prevailed. The most eminent men of both political parties, and of all parts of the confederacy, laboured together to effect an adjustment; and finally, in September, 1850, under the auspices of Clay, and Cass, and Webster, and Dickenson, and Douglas, and Foote, and other distinguished men, a series of measures were matured, sanctioned by both branches of Congress, and approved by the President.

"Under this compromise, the South has performed everything that was incumbent on her. California has been admitted as a free State, Texas has been dismembered, and the slave trade in the District of Columbia has been abolished.

"The South now asks the fulfilment of the compensating covenants on the part of the North. It is true that the fugitive slave law has passed through all the forms of legislation, and now has a place among the Acts of Congress. But it is a fact, notorious to the world, that the law is a dead letter: that while it keeps the promise to the ear, it hath broken it to the hope.

From the time of its passage to the present hour, the people, the legislative assemblies, and the judicial tribunals of the Northern States, have manifested the most determined purpose to set it at naught. Although it has been adjudged by the highest Court of the United States to be in conformity with the Constitution, and therefore to be a part of the supreme law of the land, the legislatures of almost all the Northern States have passed acts to nullify or evade its practical execution. Many of their courts have interposed every obstacle in their power to its enforcement, and mobs have risen in most of the Northern cities to resist the law, and to rescue the fugitives from labour by force of arms; and several Southern citizens have been murdered whilst engaged in attempts to arrest their slaves.

"In 1854, a bill was introduced into Congress, under the auspices of a distinguished senator from Illinois, for the organisation of territorial governments in Kansas and Nebraska. As originally reported, the bill was silent in regard to slavery. Subsequently, the bill was modified so as to embrace a clause which declared the law of 1820—commonly known as the Missouri Compromise Act—inoperative and void; and in this form it became a law. The avowed object of the mover and friends of the bill was to remove the slavery agitation from the halls of Congress, and to localise it, by confining it to the territories as they should respectively be in a condition to establish their own municipal institutions. The bill declared on its face that its true intent and meaning was 'not to legislate slavery into any territory or State, nor to exclude it therefrom, but to leave the people thereof perfectly free to form and regulate their domestic institutions in their own way, subject only to the Constitution of the United States.'

" The passage of this law furnished the pretext for the revival, with increased bitterness, of all the sectional feuds which had been temporarily allayed by the measures of 1850. Throughout the Northern States, old party lines were almost obliterated, and a new Northern political organisation sprang into existence, under the designation of the Republican party. This organisation was distinctly sectional in its character, and it soon acquired the ascendancy in almost every Northern State. The ostensible object of this party was to organise public opinion in opposition to the repeal of the Missouri Compromise, and to the extension of slavery into new territories. But it soon became evident, from the sectional character of the party, the doctrines which it inculcated, and the policy which it pursued, that its real purpose was to make war upon the institution of slavery itself. Your committee have no doubt that the ulterior designs of the leaders of the party were carefully concealed from the great body of those who enlisted under its banner, and who would have then recoiled from the idea of invading the acknowledged rights of the Southern States, and trampling under foot the solemn compacts of the Constitution. The object was to obtain the co-operation of the Northern people, by the specious pretences of opposition to the repeal of the Missouri Compromise and to the extension of slavery, and then, by the force of party affinities and discipline, to lead or drive them into open warfare on the institution itself.

"By the laws of Maine it is provided, that if a fugitive slave shall be arrested, he shall be defended by the attorney for the Commonwealth, and all expenses of such defence paid out of the public treasury. The use of all state and county gaols, and of all buildings belonging to the State, are forbidden the reception or securing fugitive slaves; and all officers are forbidden, under heavy penalties, from arresting or aiding in the arrest of such fugitives. If a slaveholder, or other person, shall unlawfully seize or confine a fugitive slave, he shall be liable to be imprisoned for not more than five years, or fined not exceeding $1000. If a slaveholder take a slave into the State, the slave is thereby made free; and if the master undertake to exercise any control over him, he is subjected to imprisonment for not less than one year, or fined not exceeding $1000.

" The Dred Scott decision of the Supreme Court has been declared unconstitutional, and many offensive and inflammatory resolutions have been passed by the Legislature.

"Vermont law now forbids all citizens and officers of the State from executing or assisting to execute the fugitive slave law, or to arrest a fugitive slave, under penalty or imprisonment for not less than one year, or a fine not exceeding $1000. It also forbids the use of all public gaols and buildings for the purpose of securing such slaves. The attorneys for the State are directed, at public expense, to defend, and procure to be discharged, every person arrested as a fugitive slave. The *habeas corpus* act also provides that fugitive slaves shall be tried by jury, and interposes other obstacles to the execution of the fugitive slave law.

"The law further provides, that all persons unlawfully capturing, seizing or confining a person as a fugitive slave, shall be confined in the State prison not more that ten years, and fined not exceeding $1000. Every person held as a slave, who shall be brought into the State, is declared free; and all persons who shall hold or attempt to hold as a slave any person so brought into that State, in any form or for any time, however short, shall be confined in the State prison not less than one nor more than fifteen years, and fined not exceeding $2000.

"The laws of Massachusetts forbid, under heavy penalties, her citizens, and State and county officers, from executing the fugitive slave law, or from arresting a fugitive slave, or from aiding in either; and denies the use of her gaols and public buildings for such purposes.

"The Governor is required to appoint commissioners in every county to aid fugitive slaves in recovering their freedom, when proceeded against as fugitive slaves, and all costs attending such proceedings are directed to be paid by the State.

"Any person who shall remove, or, attempt to remove, or come into the State with the intention to remove or assist in removing any person who is not a fugitive slave within the meaning of the Constitution, is liable to punishment by fine not less than $1000 nor more than $5000, and imprisonment not less than one nor more than five years.

"Connecticut.—By the Act of 1854, Sec. 1, it is provided, that every person who shall falsely and maliciously declare, represent, or pretend that any person entitled to freedom is a slave, or owes service or labour to any person or persons, with intent to procure or to aid or assist in procuring the forcible removal of such free person from this State as a slave, shall pay a fine of $5000, and shall be imprisoned five years in the State prison.

" 'Sect. 2. In all cases arising under this act, the truth of any declaration, representation or pretence that any person being or having been in this State, is or was a slave, or owes or did owe service or labour to any other person or persons, shall not be deemed proved except by the testimony of at least two credible witnesses testifying to facts directly tending to the truth of such declaration, pretence or representation, or by legal evidence equivalent thereto.'

" Sec. 3 subjects to a fine of $5000 and imprisonment in the State prison for five years all who shall seize any person entitled to freedom, with intent to have such person held in slavery.

" Sec. 4 prohibits the admission of depositions in all cases under this act, and provides that if any witness testifies falsely *in behalf of the party accused* and prosecuted under this act, he shall be fined $5000 and imprisoned for five years in the State prison.   This law is, in the opinion of your committee, but little short of an invitation to perjury, by imposing no penalties for false swearing *against* the party accused.

" The statutes of Rhode Island provide that any one who transports, or causes to be transported by land or water, any person lawfully inhabiting therein, to any place without the limits of the State, except by due course of law, shall be imprisoned not less than one nor more than ten years. They also prohibit all officers from aiding in executing the fugitive slave law, or arresting a fugitive slave, and deny the use of her gaols and public buildings for securing any such fugitive.

" New York has enacted that every person who shall, without lawful authority, remove'or attempt to remove from this State any fugitive slave, shall forfeit to the party aggrieved $500, and be imprisoned not exceeding ten years in the State prison ; and all accessories after the fact are also liable to imprisonment.

" The *habeas corpus* act provides that fugitive slaves shall be entitled to trial by jury, and makes it the duty of all commonwealth's attorneys to defend fugitive slaves at the expense of the State.

" New Jersey law provides that if any person shall forcibly take away from this State any man, woman, or child, bond or free, into another State, he shall be fined not exceeding $1000, or by imprisonment at hard labour not exceeding five years, or both.

" The *habeas corpus* act gives a trial by jury to fugitive slaves, and all judicial officers are prohibited from acting under any other than the law of New Jersey.

"Prior to 1847, non-resident owners of slaves were allowed to retain them in Pennsylvania not exceeding six months. In 1847 this privilege was revoked. It is further provided by law, that any person 'who violently and tumultuously seizes upon any negro or mulatto, and carries such negro away to any place, either with or without the intention of taking such negro before a district or circuit judge, shall be fined not exceeding $1000, and imprisoned in the county gaol not exceeding three months. The law also punishes with heavy fine and imprisonment in the penitentiary, any person who may forcibly carry away, or attempt to carry away, any free negro or mulatto from the States.

"Illinois has prohibited, under pain of imprisonment of not less than one nor more than seven years, any person from stealing or arresting any slave, with the design of taking such slave out of the State, without first having established his claim thereto, according to the laws of the United States. These penalties will be incurred by the master who pursues his slave across the border, and apprehends him without waiting for the action of commissioner or courts.

"The laws of Michigan are peculiarly obnoxious to criticism. They not only deny the use of the gaols and public buildings to secure fugitive slaves, and require the attorneys for the Commonwealth to defend them at the expense of the State, but the law of Connecticut in relation to the punishment of persons falsely alleging others to be slaves, is adopted, with the addition that any person who carries a slave into this

State, claiming him as such, shall be punished by imprisonment in the State prison for a period not exceeding ten years, or by a fine not exceeding $1000.

"Following the example of her sister States of the North, in parts of their hostile legislation, Wisconsin has, in some particulars, gone beyond all the rest. She has directed her district attorneys, in all cases of fugitive slaves, to appear for and defend them at the expense of the State. She has required the issue of the writ of *habeas corpus*, on the mere statement of the district attorney that a person in custody is detained as a fugitive slave, and directs all her judicial and executive officers who have reason to believe that a person is about to be arrested or claimed on such ground, to give notice to the district attorney of the county where the person resides. If a judge, in vacation, fails to discharge the arrested fugitive slave on *habeas corpus*, an appeal is allowed to the next circuit court. Trial by jury is to be granted at the election of either party, and all costs of trial, which would otherwise fall on the fugitive, are assumed by the State. A law has also been enacted, similar to that of Connecticut, for the punishment of one who shall falsely and maliciously declare a person to be a fugitive slave, with intent to aid in procuring the forcible removal of such person from the State as a slave. A section is added to the provisions of this Connecticut law, for the punishment, by imprisonment in the State prison, of any person who shall obstruct the execution of a warrant issued under it, or aid in the escape of the person accused. Another section forbids the en-

forcement of a judgment recovered for violation of the
' fugitive slave act,' by the sale of any real or personal
property in the State, and makes its provisions applicable
to judgments theretofore rendered.

" The law relative to kidnapping punishes the forcible
seizure, without lawful authority, of any person of colour,
with intent to cause him to be sent out of the State or
sold as a slave, or in any manner to transfer his service
or labour, or the actual selling or transferring the service
of such person, by imprisonment in the State prison from
one to two years, or by fine from $500 to $1000.
The consent of the party seized, sold or transferred, not
to be a defence, unless it appear to the jury that it was
not obtained by fraud, nor extorted by duress or by
threats.

" Your committee also refer to the offensive tone of a
portion of the Northern press and pulpit, and to the
libellous resolutions of numerous popular assemblies in
the Northern States, as evidences of the decline of that
spirit of fraternity and unity which animated our fathers
in the days of our revolutionary struggle. These are
the ordinary channels through which public opinion
makes itself heard and felt. But it would probably be
uncharitable to the Northern people to hold them responsible for all the ravings of fanatical agitators; and
we therefore prefer to rely on those authentic manifesta-
tions of unfriendly feeling proceeding from the official
representatives of the people, and for which the consti-
tuent body is justly responsible.

" Your committee cheerfully acquit a large number of

the Northern people of any positive and active participation in these aggressions on Southern rights and interests. The recent demonstrations of popular feeling
made in some of the Northern cities, are accepted in the
spirit in which they were offered. But abstract resolutions in favour of the guarantees of the Constitution
are of no avail, unless they are followed by correspond-
ing action. As long as the conservative people of the
North remain passive, and permit agitators and fanatics
and enemies of the South to fill positions of public
trust, and to speak and to act on behalf of their respective States, they cannot escape the responsibility which
attaches to their declarations and acts. Those who
have it in their power to prevent the perpetration of a
wrong, and fail to exercise that power, must to a great
extent be responsible for the wrong itself.

" Thus the conservative men of the North are responsible for the organisation and action of the Republican party. It was their duty to have prevented it, and
they had the power to fulfil that duty. They preferred,
however, to remain inactive, and thus permitte the Republican party to obtain the ascendancy in the State and
national councils. They could not have been ignorant
of the fact that such an organisation must necessarily
prove dangerous to the Union. They must have foreseen
that a party organised on the basis of hostility to slavery
extension, would very soon become a party opposed to
slavery itself. The whole argument against the *extension* of slavery is soon, by a very slight deflection, made
to bear against the *existence* of slavery, and thus the

anti-extension idea is merged in that of abolition. Accordingly we find, notwithstanding the denial by the Republican party of any purpose to interfere with slavery where it exists, that the tendency of its policy is to its extermination everywhere.

" The logical consequences of their teachings have been exhibited in the recent raid at Harper's Ferry ; and so long as that party maintains its present sectional organisation, and inculcates its present doctrines, the South can expect nothing less than a succession of such traitorous attempts to subvert its institutions and to incite its slaves to rapine and murder. The crimes of John Brown were neither more nor less than practical illustrations of the doctrines of the leaders of the Republican party. The very existence of such a party is an offence to the whole South.

" Your committee have no appeals or remonstrances to address to their fellow-citizens of the North. They doubtless comprehend their obligations under the Constitution to the people of the South. If they shall in future show a readiness to fulfil those obligations, Virginia and the other Southern States are prepared to bury the past in oblivion, and to respond with cordiality to every manifestation of a returning spirit of fraternity. As Virginia was among the foremost in the struggle for national independence, and contributed as much as any other State to the formation of the Constitutional Union, she would be among the last to abandon it, provided its obligations be faithfully observed. Her sons having been educated to cherish ' a cordial, habitual, and immovable attachment to our national Union—accustomed to think and to speak of it as the palladium of their political safety and prosperity, watching for its preservation with jealous anxiety, discountenancing whatever may suggest even a suspicion that it may in any event be abandoned, and indignantly frowning upon the first dawning of every attempt to alienate any portion of our country from the rest, or to enfeeble the sacred ties which now link together the various parts.'

" But the Union which they have been taught to love and revere is the Union contemplated by the Constitution—a Union of communities having equal rights—a Union regulated and governed by the principles of the Constitution—a Union of sovereign States, entitled to regulate their domestic affairs in their own way, and bound to fulfil their obligations to each other with scrupulous fidelity. When it shall cease to be such a Union, it will have forfeited all claims to their respect and affection. Virginia feels that she has discharged her wholy duty to her sister States, and she asks nothing from them that is not guaranteed to her by the plain terms of the federal compact. She has not sought officiously to intermeddle with the domestic concerns of other States, and she demands that they shall refrain from all interference with hers.

" But it is clear, from the review of the condition of the public sentiment of the Northern States for the last five years, as indicated by their legislation and in other authentic forms, that many of their people have ceased to respect the rights of the Southern States, to recognise the obligations of the federal compact, or to cherish for us those friendly sentiments which gave birth to the Constitution of the United States. A proper sense of self-respect and the instinct of preservation, therefore, require that we should adopt such measures as may be necessary to secure ourselves against future aggression, and to meet every emergency which may hereafter arise. We desire nothing but friendly relations with our sister states of the North. We ask of them nothing to which they have not solemnly bound themselves by the compact of the Constitution. But we understand our rights, and we are resolutely determined to maintain them. We disclaim all aggressive purposes. But when we are threatened with the knife of the assassin and torch of the incendiary, we cannot fold our arms in blind security. We have no desire to rupture the political, commercial, or social ties which bind us to the North, so long as our rights are respected; but, admonished by the past, it is our duty to prepare for the future by placing ourselves in an attitude of defence, and by adopting such measures as may be necessary for our security and welfare."

APPENDIX III.

Summary of Jefferson Davis' Address, June 21, 1861.

" The aggressive movements of the enemy have induced prompt and energetic action. The accumulation of the enemy's forces on the Potomac has been sufficiently demonstrative that his efforts are directed against Virginia, and from no point could the necessary measures for her protection be so efficiently directed as from our capital. The rapid progress of the last few months has stripped the veil behind which the true policy and purposes of Mr. Lincoln's Government had been previously concealed, and they are now fully revealed. The message of their President, the action of their Congress during its present session, confess the intention of subjugating the seceded States by war, a folly which is only equalled by its wickedness — a war by which it is impossible to attain the proposed result. While its dire calamities cannot be avoided by us, they will fall with redoubled severity on themselves.

" Commencing in March last with an affectation of ignorance of the secession of the seven States which organised the Confederate Government ; persisting in April in absurd assumptions of the existence of a riot which was to be dispersed by a *posse comitatus ;* continuing in successive months false representations that the States intended offensive war, in spite of conclusive evidence to the contrary, furnished as well by official action as by the basis of the Constitution, the President of the United States succeeded in deluding the people of those States into the belief that the purpose of this Government was not peace at home, but conquest abroad; not the defence of their liberties, but the subjugation of the people of the United States.

" The series of manœuvres by which the impression was created, the acts by which they were devised, and the perfidy by which they were executed, are already known. Could it be supposed they would make openly their success a subject of boast and self-laudation in the Executive Message?

" Fortunately for truth, Mr. Lincoln's Message minutely details the attempt to reinforce Fort Sumpter in violation of the armistice, of which he confesses to have been informed only by rumour too vague and uncertain to create any attention. Hostile attempts to supply Fort Sumpter are admitted to have been undertaken with a knowledge that their success was impossible. The sending a notice to the Governor of South Carolina of the intended *ruse* for the accomplishment of this object, and, quoting from the inaugural, that there would be no conflict unless these States were the aggressors, and proceeding to declare that his conduct, as in the past will. be for the future, was in performance of this promise, which could not be misunderstood. In defiance of our statement that he gave notice of the approach of a hostile fleet, he charges these States with being the assailants of the Union. The world cannot misunderstand this unfounded pretence.

" Mr. Lincoln expresses concern that some foreign nations have so shaped their action as if they supposed the early destruction of the Union probable. He abandons further disguise, and proposes to make the contest short and decisive, and confesses that even an increased force is demanded. These enormous preparations are a distinct avowal that the United States are engaged in a conflict with a great and powerful nation, and are compelled to abandon the pretence of dispersing rioters and suppressing insurrection, and are driven to the acknowledgment that the Union is dissolved. They recognise the separate existence of the Confederate States by indirection, by embargo, and blockade, by which all communication between the two is cut off. They repudiate the foolish idea that the inhabitants of the Confederacy are still citizens of the United States, for they are now waging an indiscriminate war upon them with a savage ferocity unknown to modern civilisation.

" Mr. Davis then compares the present invasion to that of Great Britain in 1781, but which was conducted in a more civilised manner.

" Mankind will shudder at the outrages committed on defenceless women by those pretending to be our fellow-citizens. Who will depict the horror with which they will regard the deliberate malignity which, under pretext of suppressing an insurrection, makes special war upon sick women and children, by carefully devised measures to prevent their obtaining medicines necessary to their cure? The sacred claims of humanity, respected by all nations, even in the fury of battle, by careful deviation of attack from hospitals, are now outraged by the Government which pretends a desire to continue a fraternal connection. Such outrages admit of no retaliation, unless the actual perpetrators are required. Taylor's mission to Washington was to propose an exchange of prisoners taken on the privateer Savannah, and to inform Mr. Lincoln that we are determined to check all barbarities on prisoners of war by such retaliation as will effectually put an end to such practices. Mr. Lincoln's promised reply has not been received.

" Reference is made to the peculiar position existing between the Confederate Government and the States usually termed border slave States, which, the Message says, cannot be properly withheld from notice. Our people are animated by the sentiments towards the inhabitants of those States which found expression in your enactment refusing to consider them enemies, or to authorise hostilities against them. That a large portion of those States regard us as brethren, and, if unrestrained by the actual presence of large armies, the subversion of the civil authority, and declaration of martial law, would some of them at least, joyfully unite with us; but that they are with almost entire unanimity opposed to the prosecution of the war waged against us, is a fact of which daily recurring events warrants the assertion. The President of the United States, in refusing to recognise those of our late sister States refraining from an attack upon us, justifies his refusal by the assertion that the States have no other power than that reserved to them in the Union by the Constitution. This new constitutional relation between the States and the general Government is a fitting introduction to another assertion of the Message — that the Executive possesses the power of suspending the writ of *habeas corpus*, and of delegating that power to military commanders, at discretion. Both these propositions claim respect equal to that which is felt for an additional statement of opinion in the same paper — that it is proper, in order to execute the laws, that the single law made to meet the extreme tenderness of citizens for liberty, so that practically it relieves more of the guilty than of the innocent, should, to a very limited extent, be violated. We may well rejoice that we have for ever severed our connection with a Government that thus tramples upon all principles of constitutional liberty, and with a people in whose presence such avowals could be paraded.

" In my message delivered in April last, I referred to the promise of abundant crops by which we were cheered. The grain crops generally have since been harvested, and the yield has been the most abundant known in our history. Many believe the supply adequate to two years' consumption for our population. Cotton, sugar, and tobacco forming the surplus production of our agriculture, and furnishing the basis of our commercial interests, present a most cheering promise, and kind Providence has smiled on the labour which extracts the teeming wealth of our soil in all portions of our Confederacy.

" It is the more gratifying to be able to give you this information, because of the need of large and increased expenditure in support of the army. Elevated and purified by the sacred cause they maintain, our fellow-citizens of every condition of life exhibit a most self-sacrificing devotion. They manifest laudable pride in upholding their independence, unaided by any resources other than their own, and the immense wealth which a fertile soil and genial climate have accumulated in this Confederacy. The patriotism of the agriculturists could not be more strikingly displayed than in the large revenues which, with eager hearts, they have zealously contributed, at the call of their country, in the single article of cotton.

" The subscriptions to the loan proposed by the government cannot fall short of $50,000,000, and will probably largely exceed that sum, and scarcely an article required for the Confederate army is provided otherwise than by subscriptions to produce a loan so happily devised by your wisdom.

" The Secretary of the Treasury, in his report submitted to you, will give you explicit details connected with that branch of the public service.

" But it is not alone in their prompt pecuniary contributions that the noble race of freemen who inhabit these States evince how worthy they are of those liberties which they so well know how to defend. When their numbers far exceed the call authorised by your laws, they have pressed the tender of their services against the enemy ; their attitude of calm and sublime devotion to their country, the cool and confident courage with which they are already preparing to meet the thousands of invaders, whatever proportions it may assume, the assurance that their sacrifices will be renewed from year to year with unfailing purpose, until they have made good to the uttermost their right to self-government, the generous and almost unquestioning confidence which they have displayed towards their Government during the pending struggle — all combine to present a spectacle such as the world has hardly, if ever seen.

" To speak of subjugating such a people, so united and determined, is to speak a language incomprehensible to them; to resist an attack upon their rights or their liberties is with them an instinct. Whether this war shall last one or three or five years is a problem they will leave to be solved by the enemy alone. It will last till the enemy shall have withdrawn from their borders — till their political rights, their altars and their houses are freed from invasion. Then, and then only, will they rest in peace from this struggle to enjoy the blessings which, with the favour of Providence, they have secured by the aid of their own strong hearts and ready arms."

APPENDIX IV.

Speech of the Earl of Derby, May 17th, 1861.

"For my own part I do not at all feel inclined to complain that the terms of the proclamation are either vague or unsatisfactory. It is quite impossible in a proclamation of this description to give an exact definition either of the character of a blockade or as to what is contraband of war. Nor do I complain of the proclamation for going beyond the necessities of the case. I mean as to the warning given to British subjects in regard to their taking part in privateering expeditions. The proclamation wisely and properly informs the subjects of her Majesty, that if they engage in those expeditions, whatever may be the result, they will have no right to claim the protection of this country against any penal consequences arising from their own act. I do not complain of that solemn warning being given to all her Majesty's subjects throughout the world, but there are two points on which I think it absolutely essential her Majesty's government should lose no time in coming to a thorough understanding with the government of the United States. First, with regard to this blockade. The

Northern States—I still call them the United States—
have indicated their intention of blockading the whole of
the Southern ports. Now, if they had a navy three
times as large as they have, it would be impossible for
them to blockade all those ports on the Southern coast.
No doubt they might blockade one port on one part of
the coast, and another port at another part, which would
be a proper blockade of those ports, and they would be
entitled to all the rights attending that state of blockade;
but I think it important that her Majesty's government
should not commit themselves to the doctrine of the
United States, that that would be equivalent to a universal blockade, or that that universal blockade would be
recognised by her Majesty's government, and that all her
Majesty's subjects breaking it will be liable to all the
penalties of breaking a blockade. Her Majesty's government should make it clearly understood that a mere paper
blockade, alleged to extend over a vast extent of coast
which it is impossible to blockade, will not be recognised
as valid by the British government. There is another
much more important point with respect to the construction put on privateering by Lord Brougham. My noble
and learned friend was understood to say that by the law
of nations privateering was piracy, and consequently
that the confederate States on each side would be perfectly justified, in carrying out that theory, in treating
all privateering as piracy, and punishing it accordingly.
Now, I apprehend that if there is anything more clear
than another it is that by the law of nations privateering
is not piracy; and no law can make that piracy as re-

gards the subjects of one nation which is not piracy by the general law of nations. The United States consequently must not be allowed to maintain such doctrines, and to call on her Majesty's government not to interfere. They must not strain the law so as to visit with the penalty of death, as for piracy, persons entitled to her Majesty's protection. This is a question which cannot be viewed with indifference, but must be seriously considered by the government. It is quite right that the people of this country shall be warned of their peril; but, on the other hand, it is essential that the United States shall not be induced to deny the general interpretation of international law, and to inflict upon persons engaged in privateering a penalty which has never hitherto been inflicted by that law. I know it will be said that the Northern States treat the Southern Confederacy not as having the rights of belligerents, but as mere rebels, and that, as rebels, their expeditions are liable to all the penalties of high treason. That is not the doctrine of this country, because we have declared them to be entitled to all the rights of belligerents; and the Northern States cannot be entitled to claim belligerent rights for themselves on the one hand, and on the other hand to deny them to the Southern States because they choose to treat them as rebels. Those are the two points upon which I think it is desirable that there should be no misunderstanding between her Majesty's government and the United States, namely, that we will not recognise anything but a real and effective blockade, actually enforced, neither will we recognise the doctrine, that by any declaration of the United States against the Southern States they should have the power of constituting privateering piracy, and visiting it with all the penalties that are attached to that offence."

The American Secession.

("Weekly Dispatch," August 11th, 1861.)

"TRUTH, justice, reason, is ever homogeneous and consistent. The attributes of God do not circumscribe, they corroborate and illustrate each other. Disinterested sincerity, clear, simple, unprejudiced candour, like the wisdom from above, is first pure, then peaceable — without partiality and without hypocrisy; it is

> '—— aye the same,
> Whether it win or lose the game;
> True as the dial to the sun,
> Although it be not shone upon.'

What an eager outcry Mr. Bright made against the inequalities of our representation! Yet when he was taken at his word, and the seats for Sudbury were transferred to the West Riding of Yorkshire, how transparent became the source of his clamour! It was not to equalise representation that he demanded an equitable distribution of seats, but simply to take seats from those whose politics were opposed to his, and to give them to those who agreed with him. We thought he was for peace at any price. 'Perish Nice, rather than go to war about it!' 'Let Savoy go—but save your money!' All because the Emperor of the French was the spoiler. Shift the scene of his 'political ethics'—move two thousand miles away—make the *experimentum in corpore* not a monarchy which is worth no Manchester man's regard, but a model Republic, that infallible pope of constitutions, and we find the member for Birmingham roaring for a war, a civil war—denouncing the assertion of the title to self-government—ignoring the clearest rights of subjects to choose their own rulers—exhuming Canning's pointed fallacy about the heptarchy, and calling upon all the world to help Abraham Lincoln to extinguish the independence of twelve millions of people, and of many Sovereign States, who never, for one hour, abdicated their prerogative of territorial supremacy. Orthodoxy in politics as in religion is Mr. Bright's doxy, and heterodoxy is the doxy of all who presume to have an opinion of their own.

"For our poor part, although our material senses be double, our moral sense happens only to be single. We have not two consciences divaricating like the compass when we cross the line. Ours is one and indivisible, acting on the one side of the Atlantic exactly as it does on the other, applying the rule and plumb-line of even-handed justice to all men, and thinking a human being has human rights, even although he should happen to be a planter of cotton. Within the memory of man America, by conquest, purchase, and settlement, belonged to England. Its colonists were English by birth, sub-

jects of our Crown, denizens of our country, owning
fealty to the Crown, bound by the obligations of patriotism to their fellow-countrymen, sworn, all the chief
of them, to their allegiance to this our State. We put a
tax upon their tea and a stamp upon their legal instruments, not to half the amount of the money the mother-
country had to pay for the government and protection
of the colonies, and far more than replaced by the exclusive monopoly of our home markets. A majority of
them, not extremely decided, took it into their heads to
stand upon a constitutional punctilio, at that time
ignored in the practice even of the mother-country, the
masses of whose people had no voice in the composition
of the Legislature, and, aided by the blunders of our
generals, wrested from us our most precious outlying
empire without even the pretext of any substantial
grievance, or real plea of oppression. Independence
Day is to this hour their highest festival. Of real Secessionists there were not more than two millions and a
half. Is there a man in all America who does not glory
in the declaration of Independence, from Abraham
Lincoln upward or downward? On what principle of
morality or common sense, then, can any one of them
deny the right of the Southerners to proclaim *their* independence *Now?* There are twelve millions of Secessionists. Can you bring any indictment against a whole
nation and half a continent? Slavery has, in all ages,
and in one form or other, been the normal condition of
every civilised, every barbarous State. To this hour it
prevails in a large portion of the world. The planters

did not make, but found it a domestic institution, on which are based the very structure and existence of society. Disguise it as we may, Abolitionism, the general policy of declaring slavery illegal beyond certain sections of the territory of the United States, is a virtual manifesto of emancipation, leads directly up to it. Do not let us be misunderstood. Slavery is a curse, and the people on whom history has imposed it are deeply to be pitied. The South ought long since to have raised the slaves gradually to human rights for the interest both of the owner and his chattel. But we must do as we would be done by, and judge of others as, in their circumstances, we would have done ourselves. What if you, and I, and we had been planters, depended entirely on slaves for our very existence — if our States drew their very life and being from slave-owning — what should *we* do if we found that a combination of other States, where there were no slaves employed, a mere counting of noses, ultimately to wrest what we regarded our whole property from us? Why, secede and fight for it, to be sure. But is this all? If a tax upon tea and deeds, not one-fourth part so heavy on the American colonies as the very same duty imposed by the mother-country on itself, justified rebellion, what is to be said of monopolies and protective and differential duties imposed on the South equal to a tax by the North of forty millions sterling? The New England States produce nothing, export nothing, cannot even feed or clothe themselves. The slave States not only maintain themselves, but export seventy millions worth annually of agricultural produce;

and yet by the craft of fiscal legislation are drowned in debt, while the North is wallowing in wealth. The poor debtor awakens to his danger, and struggles to shake himself free of the usurer and his per cents. The case is as plain as the nose on your face. Every colony *we* have is self-governed, self-taxed, entirely independent upon us or upon each other. We cannot even send convicts to our own property because the settlers object. We cannot even interfere with their land tenure, their chief domestic institution. *We* have allowed the United States to go from us, and find both countries to be the better for it. On what pretence can we of all nations deny the right of twelve millions of people to self-government, and to secede from a community that virtually confiscates their property, and oppresses them with unequal taxation?

"But is this all? The thirteen States which formed the original Union were each separate and independent colonies. On the 2nd July, 1776, they declared that 'they were, and of right ought to be, free and independent States, and the connection between *them* (the plural) and the *State* of Great Britain ought to be dissolved.' The declarants voted by *States*, not by populations. By the Confederation of 1778 Article II. declares that 'each State *retains* its sovereignty, freedom, and independence, and every power, jurisdiction, and right which is not by this Confederation expressly delegated to the United States.' The Confederation of 1789 was instituted by voting by *States;* the Presidency of Lincoln is that of the majority of States, not of the majority of population. Can it be for one moment contended that there is any power delegated by the several States of the Union of compelling them to remain in it after they choose to declare a dissolution of the co-partnery? What is the Union but the common foreign agent of all the States? Do they emanate from it, or does its power emanate from them? Has it any power or position of its *own*, any but that which each *delegated* to it? Is it anything but the creature of the States? Has it any separate existence?

" We are told about the heptarchy, about the cases of Ireland and of Scotland. Well — even *these* are very open to argument; and it is very certain that if the Imperial Legislature violated any of the articles of either Union, or by partial laws confiscated the property of one nation, the right of secession would lawfully and constitutionally revive. But Ireland and Scotland have no Legislatures of their own; are not sovereign States; did not *retain* by articles of union any separate sovereignty. Life and property are secured in the several American States by the separate Government and Legislature of each, not by the Union. A citizen of one State is not that of another, cannot vote in another. Every separate State has its own code of laws, its own revenues, its own debts, its own property. No two States have the same code; the citizens of each are subject to different modifications of their constitutional rights — each State has a different constitution. In 1814 the New England States threatened to secede. Massachusetts did so on the annexation of Texas. The Southern States have frequently proclaimed their resolution to do so — and this Morill Tariff, in the very crisis of dissension, would of itself form an ample justification of separation. The very fact that negroes are chattels in Louisiana, and citizens in New York; that a British subject of colour can be put in jail at New Orleans, without any offence but his skin, and that to all our remonstrances to the Government at Washington the answer is, such is the law of Louisiana, and the United States cannot interfere, is conclusive of the sovereignty of each State, and of its right to go out of the Union by the same power it had to go in. The principle involved in this quarrel is that which is put in issue in Naples, in Italy, in Hungary, in Poland. *Cælum non animam mutant qui trans mare currunt.* What is right in Europe cannot be wrong in America. We protest against the poltroonery which, out of fear of the petulant gasconade of the North, induces our contemporaries, even our Legislature, to ' sing small,' and profess that our press and our people's sympathies are all with the Northerners. We believe the case to be exactly the reverse; and the best friends of the Unionists are those who, at any hazard of provoking the insolent imperiousness of the North, tell it plainly the truth, and assert to its face the claims of justice and the manifest rights of nations. The arguments of Lincoln are the worn-out drivel of legitimacy and despotism.

" We insist on these views, because we have great faith in the ultimate triumph of what is honest — in the aphorism that ' the richt will gang the richt gait.' ' Thrice is he armed who hath his quarrel just.' When

the prospects of the South were the blackest, we said it
was invincible if it was inspired by the spirit of Washington, who, in defence of his home, with a handful of men,
defied the disciplined armies and the blockade of the
victorious navies of England. Twelve millions of people
cannot be conquered in their own country but by their
own cowardice and want of patriotism, even by bunkum notes of hundreds of millions of money, and half
million contingents of soldiers — on paper. The Federalists are invaders. They are assailing men, women,
and children, who are simply defending themselves from
undisciplined arson, rape, and murder. The Northern
Generals proclaim their own armies ruffians. Regiments
of slaves are even now found fighting on the side of their
Southern owners. Slaves who have fled do not know
how to live without a master. While blatant Yankee
fools have in Paris been boasting of their sympathy with
the despots of France and Russia, and in New York have
been howling for a war with England, while they have
been beating their breasts like gorillas to lash themselves
up to ferocity, and bragging and boasting 'enough to
make a monkey puke,' the Southerners have said nothing,
preserved their dignity as men by wise but effectual
reticence; have quietly blown up the *Times'* correspondent with *canards* and bosh, letting him apparently see
everything, and really know nothing; and steadily pursued
the policy we have frequently foreshadowed, of pretending to retreat until they had led the invaders into their
Southern territory, that they might rise up behind them.
The result is an ignominious defeat of the vapouring

gascons of the North within sight of their very capital, in a great pitched battle, and a demonstration of the utter unreality of the pretensions and the entire hollowness and treachery of all the appearances and demonstrations of the Federalists.

" The Union, the creature itself of disloyalty, rebellion, and treason, is not so old yet as many thousands of the people on both sides of the Atlantic. It is the bantling of the *philosophes* of the Encyclopædia, and has never been anything but a paper constitution, entirely unworkable when put to the test. The Republic has been sustained entirely by its federal, that is to say, its disunited character — by every separate colony having retained the power of varying its laws and constitution to suit its local character and circumstances — the very principle asserted in this secession. It has been sustained solely by yearly migrations of the most productive members of the European population, the native Americans having palpably degenerated. Common sense might tell us that a country far larger than all Europe, containing every climate from Petersburg to Calcutta, utterly diverse sympathies, character, ethnology, social institutions, and material needs, could never be really governed from one centre and by the same legislature. It is the plain interest of both North and South that they should become severally compacted by peaceable separation. It is essential to the peace of the world that such a huge confederacy, totally beyond the effectual control of the most powerful Government, should no longer be left to the nominal jurisdiction of the feeblest and most feckless.

If we would perpetuate slavery, no expedient could so secure that end as forcing back the Southerners into the Union, fenced by obsequious guarantees for the perpetuation of their peculiar domestic institution. If we would embitter strife to undying hatred, we should help the North to make a subjugated people of the Secessionists. If we would destroy far more property by war and its cost than the fee simple of all the slaves would come to, we shall counsel the pursuit of this fratricidal war. If we would perpetuate rebellion, sedition, insecurity, and uncertainty, we should wish well to a conquest that can never lead to permanent tranquillity, or to the real acceptance by the South of their humiliated subjection. If we would destroy the very principle of the Republican constitution, by an army of occupation, martial law, the hero-worship of successful military commanders, and an enormous national debt, by all means let us encourage a policy which will transfer to the new world the worst features of the effete monarchies of the old. Success would be ruin to the Republic; failure ruin to the North. Peaceable secession and equitable adjustment are equally for the interest of the belligerents, the cause of emancipation, and the future peace and liberty of the world. Already the Northern statesmen speak openly of the annexation of Canada. Already the Northern press and the vagrant stump oratory of New England counsel a war with Britain. A hundred millions of fillibusters before the century is out must either be divided among themselves, or overawe every other nation."

What the Southern States of America are Fighting for.

("London Review," August, 1861.)

"To themselves, at least, the South seems to be fighting in vindication of a great principle with which the people of England can sympathise, in spite of their hatred of slavery—a principle which lies at the root of the whole difficulty, and which is no other than the sacred right of self-government. As Sovereign States, each with its own Legislature and Government, and not as mere counties in a kingdom, or parishes in a city, the seceders claim the right to withdraw from a voluntary confederacy—a partnership from which they no longer derive any advantage, and to which they owe no allegiance or loyalty—a right which they hold to be as sacred as that right of revolt against British injustice which freed the colonies from the dominion of the mother-country. On what principle, they ask, can the North combat the proposition, unless it be that on which George III. and his advisers combated Washington? And does the North imagine that it can successfully combat the South on that issue? And if not on that issue, will it fight in vindication of that still grander principle, the emancipation of the slaves? Hitherto the North has not been Abolitionist. It has not hated slavery, but has simply desired its non-extension; and if it be not prepared, as we do not think it is, to hoist the flag of universal emancipation, and to inaugurate a holy war for the freedom of the black population, and the consequent ruin of the greatest and most productive cotton-fields in the world, it stands in a false and untenable position."

APPENDIX V.

The following is the new Tariff Act as it passed Congress : —

A Bill to provide increased revenue from imports, to pay the interest on the public debt, and for other purposes :

Be it enacted by the Senate and House of Representatives of the United States of America in Congress assembled, That from and after the date of the passage of this Act, in lieu of the duties heretofore imposed by law on the articles hereinafter mentioned, and on such as may now be exempt from duty, there shall be levied, collected, and paid on the goods, wares, and merchandise herein enumerated and provided for, imported from foreign countries, the following duties and rates of duty, that is to say: 1st. On raw sugar, commonly called Muscovado or brown sugar, and on sugars not advanced above No. 12 Dutch standard, by claying, boiling, clarifying, or other process, and on syrup of sugar or of sugar cane and concentrated molasses, or concentrated melado, 2c. per pound, and on white and clayed sugar, when advanced beyond the raw state, above No. 12

Dutch standard, by clarifying or other process, and not yet refined 2½c. per pound; on refined sugars, whether loaf, lump, crushed, or pulverised, 4c. per pound; on sugars after being refined, when they are tinctured, coloured, or in any way adulterated, and on sugar candy, 6c. per pound; on molasses 5c. per gallon. Provided that all syrups of sugar or of sugar cane, concentrated molasses or melado, entered under the name of molasses, or any other name than syrup of sugar cane, concentrated molasses, or concentrated melado, shall be liable to forfeiture to the United States. On all tea, 15c. per pound; on almonds, 4c. per pound; shelled almonds, 6c. per pound; on brimstone, crude, $3 per ton; on brimstone, in rolls, $6 per ton; on coffee of all kinds, 4c. per pound; on cocoa, 3c. per pound; on cocoa leaves and cocoa shells, 2c. per pound; on cocoa, prepared or manufactured, 8c. per pound; on chicory root, 1c. per pound; and on chicory, ground, 2c. per pound; on chocolate, 6c. per pound; on cassia, 10c. per pound; cassia buds, 15c. per pound; on cinnamon, 20c. per pound; on cloves, 8c. per pound; on cayenne pepper, 6c. per pound; on cayenne pepper, ground, 8c. per pound; on currants, 5c. per pound; on argol, 3c. per pound; on cream tartar, 6c. per pound; on tartaric acid and tartar emetic, and Rochelle salts, 10c. per pound; on dates, 2c. per pound: on figs, 5c. per pound; on ginger root, 3c. per pound; on ginger, ground, 5c. per pound; on liquorice, paste and juice, 5c. per pound; liquorice root, 1c. per pound; on mace and nutmegs, 25c. per pound; on nuts of all kinds not otherwise provided for, 2c. per pound; on pepper, 6c. per pound; on pimento, 6c. per pound; on plums, 5c. per pound; on prunes, 5c. per pound; on raisins, 5c. per pound; on unmanufactured Russian hemp, $40 per ton; on Manilla and other hemps from India, $25 per ton; on lead, in pigs or bars, $1 50c. per 100 pounds, in sheets, $2 25c. per 100 pounds, on white lead, dry or ground in oil, and red lead, $2 25c. per 100 pounds; on salt, in sacks, 18c. per 100 pounds, and in bulk, 12c. per 100 pounds; on soda ash, ½c. per pound; on bicarbonate of soda, 1c. per pound; on sal soda, ½c. per pound; on caustic soda, 1c. per pound; on chloride of lime, 30c. per 100 pounds; on saltpetre, crude, 1c. per pound; refined, or partially refined, 2c. per pound; on turpentine, 10c. per gallon; on oil of cloves, 70c. per pound; on brandy, $1 25c. per gallon; on spirits distilled from grain or other materials, 50c. per gallon; on gum copal, and other gums or resinous sub-stances used for the same or similar purposes as gum copal, 10c. per pound.

" Sect. 2. And be it further enacted, That from and after the day and year aforesaid, there shall be levied, collected, and paid, on the importation of the articles hereinafter mentioned, the following duties, that is to say : — On arrowroot, 20 per cent. ad valorem; on ginger, preserved or pickled, 30 per cent. ad valorem; on limes, lemons, oranges, bananas, and plantains, 20 per cent. ad valorem; on Peruvian bark, 15 per cent. ad valorem; on quinine, 30 per cent. ad valorem; on rags, whatever material, 10 per cent.; on gunpowder, 30 per cent. ad valorem; on feathers and down, 30 per cent. ad valorem ; on hides, 10 per cent. ad valorem ; on sole and bend leather, 30 per cent. ad valorem ; on India-rubber, raw or unmanufactured, 10 per cent. ad valorem; on India-rubber shoes and boots, 30 per cent. ad valorem ; on ivory manufactured, and on vegetable ivory, 10 per cent. ad valorem ; on wines of all kinds, 50 per cent. ad valorem ; on silk in the gum, not more advanced in the manufacture than singles, tram, and thrown or organise, 25 per cent. ad valorem ; on all silks valued at not over $1 per square yard, 30 per centum ad valorem ; on all silks valued at over $1 per square yard, 40 per cent. ad valorem ; on all silk velvets, or velvets of which silk is the component material of chief value, valued at $3 per square yard, 35 per cent. ad valorem ; valued at over $3 per square yard, 40 per cent. ad valorem ; on floss silks, 30 per cent. ad valorem ; on silk ribbons, galloons, braids, fringes, laces, tassels, buttons, button cloths, trimmings, and on silk twist, twist composed of mohair and silk, sewing silk in the gum or purified, and all other manu-factures of silk, or of which silk shall be the component material of chief value, not otherwise provided for, 40 per cent. ad valorem.

" Sect. 3. And be it further enacted, That all articles, goods, wares, and merchandise, imported from beyond the Cape of Good Hope in foreign vessels, not entitled by reciprocal treaties to be exempt from discriminating duties, tonnage and other charges, and all other articles, goods, wares and merchandise not imported direct from the place of growth or production, or in foreign vessels entitled by reciprocal treaties to be exempt from discriminating duties, tonnage, and other charges, shall be subject to pay, in addition to the duties imposed by this Act, 10 per cent. ad valorem. Provided, That this rule shall not apply to goods, wares, and merchandise imported from beyond the Cape of Good Hope in American vessels.

"Sect. 4. And be it further enacted, That from and after the passage of this Act, there shall be allowed on all articles wholly manufactured of materials imported, on which duties have been paid, when exported, a drawback equal in amount to the duty paid on such materials and no more, to be ascertained under such regulations as shall be prescribed by the Secretary of the Treasury. Provided, That 10 per cent. on the amount of all drawbacks so allowed, shall be retained for the use of the United States, by the collectors paying such drawbacks, respectively. ·

"Sect. 5. And be it further enacted, That all goods, wares, and merchandise, actually on shipboard and bound to the United States, and all goods, wares, and merchandise, on deposit in warehouses or public stores at the date of the passage of this Act, shall be subject to pay such duties as are provided by law before and at the time of the passage of this Act. And provided further, That all goods deposited in public store or bonded warehouse after this Act takes effect and goes into operation if designed for consumption in the United States, must be withdrawn therefrom, or the duties thereon paid in three months after the same are deposited, and goods designed for exportation and consumption in foreign countries may be withdrawn by the owner at any time before the expiration of three years after the same are deposited, such goods, if not withdrawn in three years, to be regarded as abandoned to the Government, and sold under such regulations as the Secretary of the Treasury may prescribe, and the proceeds paid into the Treasury. Provided, That merchandise, upon which the owner may have neglected to pay duties within three months from the time of its deposit, may be withdrawn and entered for consumption at any time within two years of the time of its deposit, upon the payment of the legal duties, with an addition of 25 per cent. thereto. Provided also, That merchandise upon which duties have been paid, if exported to a foreign country within three years, shall be entitled to return duties, proper evidence of such merchandise having been landed abroad to be furnished to the collector by the importer, 1 per cent. of said duties to be retained by the Government.

"Sect. 6. And be it further enacted, That the Act entitled 'An Act to provide for the payment of outstanding treasury notes, to authorise a loan, to regulate and fix the duties on imports, and for other purposes,' approved March 2, 1861, be, and the same is hereby, amended as follows, that is to say: first, in Section 6, article 1st, after the words 'in cordials and' strike out 'liquors' and insert 'liqueurs;' second, in the same section, after the word 'represent,' insert 'Provided also, that no lower rate or amount of duty shall be levied, collected, and paid on brandy, spirits, and all other spirituous beverages, than that now fixed by law for the description of first proof, but shall be increased in proportion for any greater strength than the strength of first proof;' third, Section 12, article 1st, after the words ' 18 cents,' where they first occur, insert ' or less;' fourth, Section 13, article 2nd, after the word ' manufacturer,' insert 'except hosiery ;' fifth, in the same section, article 3rd, strike out ' wool' wherever it occurs, and insert in each place 'worsted;' sixth, in Section 14, article 1st, after the words ' ten per centum,' insert 'ad valorem ;' seventh, in Section 15, before the word 'yarns,' insert ' hemp;' in the same section, after the word 'sheetings,' insert 'of flax or hemp,' and strike out 'jute goods,' and in lieu thereof insert 'jute yarns;' eighth, in Section 22, strike out the words ' unwrought clay, $3 per ton;' ninth, in Section 19, strike out 'compositions of glass or paste not set, intended for use by jewellers ;' tenth, in Section 22, strike out 'compositions of glass or paste when set;' eleventh, in Section 23, article sheathing metal, strike out 'yard,' and insert 'foot;' in Section 7, clause 5th, the words 'on screws washed or plated, and all other screws, of iron or any other metal,' shall be stricken out, and the words 'on screws of any other metal than iron' shall be inserted.

" Sect. 7. And be it further enacted, That all Acts and parts of Acts repugnant to the provisions of this Act be, and the same are hereby, repealed : Provided, that the existing laws shall extend to, and be in force for, the collection of the duties imposed by this Act for the prosecution and punishment of all offences, and for the recovery, collection, distribution, and remission of all fines, penalties, and forfeitures, as fully and effectually as if every regulation, penalty, forfeiture, provision, clause, matter, and thing to that effect in the existing laws contained, had been inserted in and re-enacted by this Act.

APPENDIX VI.

I SEE by the Board of Trade returns, that in six items of exports alone, the United States lost in the month of June 1861, 534,862*l*., and the British North American colonies gained 144,947*l*., viz. cotton, earthenware, haberdashery, hardware, iron, and woollen stuffs.

THE END.

LONDON
PRINTED BY SPOTTISWOODE AND CO.
NEW-STREET SQUARE

www.ingramcontent.com/pod-product-compliance
Lightning Source LLC
Chambersburg PA
CBHW020936120726

47905CB00008B/2539